COFFEE, MARTINIS,
and
SAN FRANCISCO

RUTH BRANSTEN McDOUGALL

COFFEE, MARTINIS,
and
SAN FRANCISCO

RUTH BRANSTEN McDOUGALL

Presidio Press
San Rafael, California / London, England

Published by Presidio Press of San Rafael, California,
and London, England, with editorial offices at
1114 Irwin Street, San Rafael, California

Library of Congress Cataloging in Publication Data

McDougall, Ruth Bransten.
    Coffee, martinis, and San Francisco.

    1. Bransten, Manfred.   2. Brandenstein (M. J.)
and Company, San Francisco—History.   3. San
Francisco—History.   4. Businessmen—United
States—Biography.   I. Title.
HD9199.U48B75   338'.092'4 [B]   78-17880
ISBN 0-89141-039-2

Book design by Hal Lockwood

Jacket design by John Hunt

Printed in the United States of America

To
Brother Joe
and
my grandchildren

CONTENTS

ACKNOWLEDGMENTS

I wish to express my appreciation to all those who helped me along the rocky road that leads between ideas and getting them down on paper: Adele Horwitz, my agent, who encouraged and guided me; Joan Griffin, my editor, for her wise suggestions; and my brother Joe, a walking book of knowledge on our early days in San Francisco. Also to John van der Zee for his descriptions of the Bohemian Grove encampments.

Mannie

I

JAPANESE UNDERSTAND EARTHQUAKES

"*MANFRED DEAR,* wear your hat!"

Renée was leaning from the second-floor window in a batiste nightgown, whose prim collar was in stark contrast to the unpinned hair falling over her shoulders. She was calling in controlled but urgent tones to Mannie, her husband, as he darted out into the street. His balding head was faintly luminous in the early spring morning. He started to board a lurching dray as it clattered by the house on Sacramento Street, but he was fended off and paused for a moment while his wife's voice, cool and clear above the clamor, floated down to him once more.

"Manfred, you'll catch cold!"

The street, usually a quiet residential oasis in still-lusty San Francisco, was choked with traffic. Private carriages, delivery wagons, carts, and an occasional automobile overflowed with businessmen trying to get to the downtown area. The passengers, hastily attired in dark suit coats and trousers with nightshirts and long underwear gaping and flapping, looked more like guests on their way to a come-as-you-are costume ball than sedate men of affairs. The attempts of some to dignify their appearance with the addition of stovepipe or bowler only added a bizarre touch to the chaotic scene.

Recollecting that his hat was still in his hand, Mannie crammed his derby over his head and lunged for the running board of a wagon a little less jampacked with fugitives than the rest. From this steep-pitched angle, his derby was nearly knocked off by a shower of brick that fell into the street. Recovering his balance, he waved one hand and roared to the watching woman on the second floor, "Pack, I'll be back with an automobile!" How, he had no idea. First he had to get to his beloved office.

It was six o'clock in the morning of April 18, 1906. San Francisco was on fire! For those interminable moments one hour before, San Francisco had done the bumps and grinds in terrorizing imitation of the Barbary Coast dance hall girls accompanied with the deep rush of protesting masonry that only the earthquake-wise know.

I was too young to remember this. My brother and I had slept peacefully while the house rocked and shuddered and the chimney added its rubble to the street. Yet the story of those moments was so often retold by my parents that they now seem part of my memory. When the pitching stopped, Renée came in and reassured herself about our immediate safety.

"Earthquakes or no, the children's routine is not to be disturbed," she told herself. We were to sleep until seven o'clock as usual!

Mannie, my father, his voice a little off-key, ordered Renée to dress immediately and take the family to safe refuge in Alta Plaza Park, just around the corner. He had then reached for his derby and charged out of the house, shouting further instructions from the wagon as it headed for a right-

of-way through less-crowded streets. Had Mannie stayed longer he might have seen the French maid-of-all-work, wrapped
in a feather boa, taking flight down the front steps and shrill-
ing: *"Mon Dieu! Mon Dieu! La fin du monde!"* But his mind
was on his office in the MJB building across town. He and his
brother Max had taken a heavy gamble by locating a growing
coffee, tea, and rice business at Spear and Mission, and he had
to get there fast.

He was too impatient to stay on the lumbering wagon.
The talk was that riots had already started. The quake had
burst the water mains, and the fire department was nearly
powerless to check the blaze. Unheeding, Mannie jumped
down and ran. He ran across Market Street, past police barricades, wavering between hope one moment and a sense of
futility the next. Some buildings were untouched by the
quake. What would he find at Spear and Mission? His usual
optimistic nature was at a temporary loss. Could anything
survive such an inferno? All around, other buildings stood
broken, sliding into rubble, shattered. The few survivors were
like monuments to a lost race. Through the billowing black
smoke, he glimpsed the MJB building near the Southern Pacific yards. His heart jumped with relief. As he reached the
corner, relief plummeted to despair. He saw a shell, a naked
steel outline, warped and twisted by the earth's convulsions.
The stone had crumbled and flames had gutted the interior.
He pushed by the few firemen left on the scene and leaned
against a half-ruined wall. Nausea from the fumes and fear
swept over him. "Gone, all gone!" he said to himself. His
mind flashed to his wife and family whom he had left at Sacramento Street. They were safe where they were.

Safe! Why hadn't he remembered? Surely the MJB safe,
where all the accounts and checks were kept, was fireproof!

Stepping over the smoldering sacks of green coffee beans,
sacks of charred rice and spilled tea, Mannie managed to
make his way to the back office where the safe was kept.

Hope surging, he opened the door. Instead of a safe by the far wall, he saw a gaping hole in the floor. He looked down. The safe rested between two flaming rafters. He resisted an impulse to jump through the fiery hole. Putting a handkerchief over his nose, he ran to the iron steps leading to the basement. A blast of fresh air swept against his face. It came from a modern improvement, a tube which carried air from upstairs to the lower floor. It had done a remarkable job, so intensifying the heat that the front of the safe was already melting like lava. Some of the contents had spilled to the ground.

Mannie bent down to pick up a partially burned ledger and was summarily ordered aside by two firemen. The last thing Mannie saw on the ledger were the letters M. J. Brandenstein and Co., 1881, vaporizing in the yellow ember glow. Hopeless, he clambered back over the debris to the front of the building. A voice hailed him. It was his brother Max.

"No use, Max. We can do nothing here."

The brothers looked at one another, then stood shoulder to shoulder before the smoking ruin. The structure was barely two years old. It represented all of their capital and their dream of building the largest importing firm on the West Coast. Despite warnings from Pa Brandenstein, their father, the brothers had borrowed heavily to build the office and warehouse for the expanding tea, rice, and coffee business. Max, the oldest son, was looking at Mannie as if feeling the whole weight of the loss. Could anything be done at all? Would Pa help? No, it wouldn't be fair to expect Pa, no longer active in the business, to pull their coffee beans out of the fire for them. Max watched Mannie who was standing ankle deep in wet ashes trying to right an overturned desk.

"Why bother with a desk at a time like this?" he protested.

"Give me a hand," Mannie replied. "There's something

important in the middle drawer—the last big order we got from Kamikowa Brothers. I meant to put it in the safe, then forgot."

With Max's help the desk was brought to an upright position. Mannie pulled at a drawer jammed by heat and water. "I can't remember the exact amount of the order, but it was close to fifteen thousand. They're our biggest Japanese importers in California."

Max shook his head. "As if I didn't know. Here," he said, handing Mannie a pocketknife, "try this."

Mannie jabbed at the drawer partition and yanked the handle. The drawer remained shut as if it had been sealed with a Yale lock.

Max placed his chubby arms around Mannie's slender waist, and together they tugged. Unexpectedly the drawer yielded, tumbling its contents and the brothers onto the floor. They were surrounded by a mass of soaked papers, runny glue, and a bottle of spilled ink. Mannie started to laugh.

"How can you laugh, Mannie?" Max reached for a tissue letter sheet on which the words Kamikowa Brothers stood out clearly. All the rest was a blotch of print.

"I can't help it, Max. We look more like the Katzenjammer kids than the two senior partners of M. J. Brandenstein."

"You can say that again! Has the earthquake unsettled your minds?" Max and Mannie got up from the floor to see their brother Eddie staring at them in disbelief. Now Charlie, their youngest brother, came through the shattered door, shouting, "How bad is it? Nobody ever tells me anything!"

Mannie grimly explained the loss of the order, adding, "Look boys, that's just one order. Copies of all the rest are in the safe. With the condition the safe's in, they might as well be at the bottom of the Pacific. Let's face it. Unless the customers come through, we're broke."

The four brothers and business associates took stock

again of the ruined building. Nothing could be salvaged in a material sense. They had to set their sights on the future. But what could the future hold for a business deeply in debt?

A gruff voice behind said, "You have me left."

It was Pa Brandenstein. A cigar clenched in his teeth, he raised his arms and thrust them around the shoulders of his sons who stood in a huddle, heads bent.

"Temporarily, you can set up business at my home." He paused to spit out the chewed end of his cigar. "The old house is pretty empty with all of you away. With Ma gone it's not much like a home anyway. Yes, the thing to do is to start again at California and Gough."

The brothers stared at one another. They started to protest that there was nothing with which to start over—no money, no records, nothing but rubble.

Pa Brandenstein, usually an excitable man, drew back as if to indicate the huddle was over.

"I'll give you thirty thousand dollars," he said calmly. "You have me. You will be all right."

There could be no looking back with this sort of confidence. The family meeting broke up with the brothers seeking their individual families. Mannie had promised to return with an automobile and he was a man of his word. But plunging back into the strange world of the dispossessed San Franciscans, a world in a terrible hurry, Mannie found that securing the services of an automobile was about as easy as securing a quiet luncheon at his club. The roar of the fires, the incessant clanging of the fire trucks, the explosions from dynamiting and backfires, the shouting of lone civilians at passing traffic, had not abated; and he dived up Mission Street hailing every vehicle in sight. He had almost given up hope when a Stanley Steamer puffed to a stop. Mannie was flashing a twenty-dollar gold piece, and the driver, a tall, gaunt individual, shouted, "Hop in, mister, I can always use twenty bucks!"

Mannie tossed the gold piece to him and jumped into the seat near the driver.

"Alta Plaza Park—and hurry!"

The man shook his head. "I'm going to the Majestic Theater."

Mannie yelled, "Are you crazy, man? That's Market near Ninth. The fire's worse down there!"

"Git out if you want to, mister. I've got my twenty."

The more Mannie argued, the more the driver insisted. "I'm goin' to the Majestic, come hell or high water."

"You'll find hell all right there," Mannie retorted, "but you won't find any water."

"Listen, mister," the gaunt Stanley Steamer driver rejoined, "I don't give a damn how much this town burns. It ain't goin' to burn me out of this here machine."

He paused to chuckle, showing a row of store teeth, and went on. "An actor fellow give this machine to me to take care of while he went on tour, and the way it looks from here," he squinted his eyes against the smoke, "he won't be coming back to 'Frisco for a long time. I'll tell you something else. The fire ain't goin' to burn me out of four hundred in gold I got stashed away in a strongbox at the theater. Not if I can help it." He pressed the Klaxon. "Now, are you ridin' with me or ain't you?"

Mannie thought of the company steel safe. What chance had this man of finding his gold in a strongbox? But what was the use of arguing? Any automobile, any driver was better than none. He nodded. He could almost visualize the brick building known as the Majestic exposed to the sort of inferno to which the MJB building had succumbed. Nor were his fears groundless. When the Stanley Steamer did get there, the riders were faced by a building with the whole facade missing, and the sagging stage exposed to the smoke-filled sky. Mannie tried to stop the driver from entering the smoldering ruin. But there was no holding him. There was gold in the ashes.

Mannie waited while the minutes, like the city, burned and drifted away from him. History was telescoping itself, cramming an era into a minute, focusing its lusty life and sweeping it away. The sands were running through the hour-glass and the absurd old man searching for gold was keeping Mannie from his family. What could gold avail him? But he did emerge, with smoke-blackened face, crying, "Eureka!" He was carrying what appeared to be a sack of thick, charred cloth. Climbing into the car, his store teeth the only white spot on his face, he said with sudden affability, "I'll drive you anywhere you want now, mister!"

"Do you mean to tell me," Mannie asked on their way to Alta Plaza Park, "that your strongbox didn't melt in the fire?"

"It melted all right. But you see, I kept my gold wrapped in this here piece of carpet—cheap but tough! That's what saved my money."

Despite the swarms of people in the park, Mannie found his family and the joy of reunion temporarily wiped out his misery. By about four o'clock, when the dynamiting to stem the inexorable progress of the fire was at its height, we all piled into the Stanley Steamer—Mannie and Renée, my brother Joe, and me, a little girl who knew nothing of history or the wickedness of the Barbary Coast, and who could hardly have any regrets on leaving a temporarily stricken city.

The old man deposited his carpet-wrapped gold on the floorboard of the car, insisting on being our chauffeur for as long as we needed him. He had no home. His rooming house in the shacktown section of town had burned. He would have no job as a watchman at the Majestic.

I do not recall the drive down to Mountain View, but I do remember snatches of after-the-fire stories told by my parents. Next door to us, for instance, Mrs. Kohn's fourteen-year-old daughter Enid screamed to her mother to get up. Mrs. Kohn, terrified, refused to move. She felt safest in her bed, which rocked like a cradle. The earth gave another convulsive heave, and Enid caught the ormolu clock as it fell off the mantle, chiming.

On the other side of our home lived the Mitaus. Mr. Mitau, of German descent, deliberate and punctilious, insisted he would not leave until he had shaved. His wife's frantic pleas to hurry, hurry could be heard by all the neighbors. And throughout the confusion there was the sound of a piano being played furiously. It came through the bashed-out window of a lady down the block. She had just acquired a Steinway. Now she sat in her fur coat covering her nightgown, playing trills and obligatos as though she would never have a chance to play a piano again.

We were told that mother's sister, Aunt Jeanne, had lost her new home near Van Ness. In the path of the fire fighters, it had bowed out behind a curtain of smoke. Surprisingly, my grandparents' seemingly fragile house at the edge of Golden Gate Park had remained intact, while many of its Victorian neighbors tumbled their cupolas and littered the ground with stained glass.

The Panhandle was jammed with refugees who, under the surveillance of the militia, cooked on improvised stoves and brushed their teeth in the small stream of water from the hydrants.

I remember the hydrants for another reason. Joe, always a roamer, had earlier hiked over the hot and broken pavements all the way to Van Ness to inspect the ruins of Aunt Jeanne's house. When he returned he announced he'd seen a crazy man drink water from a hydrant nearby, beat his chest and holler, "Me, me, meee!" The wild man had been imitating Caruso, who was in San Francisco and in the same unpleasant fix as the rest of us.

In Mountain View, Mother's aunt had a cottage meant for two. I only recall lots of feet in bed. We children slept six in a bed, three heads at the top and three at the bottom. The grownups slept on the floor. Our chauffeur slept in his Stanley Steamer.

Each morning Mannie dressed carefully and was then

driven over the badly buckled roads to San Francisco, where he and his brothers met at Pa Brandenstein's house. They started to piece together the company records. From bills of lading Mannie discovered at the Southern Pacific Depot, they were able to begin again.

Mannie reserved part of the day for the search for food. He must have had some influence with the grocers, for he never returned to Mountain View empty-handed. There were tins of sardines, beans, soups, and, on one occasion, a twenty-pound ham. Fortunately, we were not orthodox; the ham disappeared as if it had been inhaled and the bone was made into soup for the children.

If the issue was ever in doubt that Mannie and his brothers, with Pa's help, could not climb back from the specter of the old MJB building, the doubt was dispelled one morning a month later when Mannie was greeted by Max, waving a telegram.

"Mannie, look at this!"

The telegram read: "Please accept fourteen thousand eight hundred dollars advance payment for last order. Japanese understand earthquakes."

It was signed, "Kamikowa Brothers, Fresno, California."

Mannie and Max hugged each other. They were shaking. It wasn't from laughter.

II

WHEN JULIE
WAS CARELESS

*T*HAT MANNIE and Renée should have married remained the mystery of my childhood. Although both
were born in San Francisco, their union was a collision
of two worlds—one German, one French.

My dad was a man of many talents: supersalesman, rac-
onteur, and would-be actor. But coffee, aside from me, was
his baby. His bushy moustache curved over full lips ever ready
to part in a smile. He was a slender, short man, whom I never
heard comment on his lack of height. I remember his telling
me, "Don't draw attention to a flaw. Others may not have
noticed it."

Renée, my mother, was tall, beautiful, and dignified. She
singed her wings continuously around the flame of Mannie's
laughter, and if her lack of response irritated him, he needed
her in the same way a funny man needs a straight one. Nor
would either of them have been quite whole without the
other. When tension mounted between them, as it often did,
Renée contained her annoyance behind compressed lips and

an air of detachment. Mannie, volatile and voluble, would accuse her with such phrases as, "If I say needles, you say pins. If I say buttons, you say shoes." And in final irritation would shout, "Pardon me for breathing!" Though quick to anger, he was also quick to regret, and next evening would arrive home with a box of juicy nectarines or some fresh bay shrimps. Dad, who couldn't speak a word of the French language and thought it sounded like "trois bleu boom boom," laughed when I would run to mother, calling, *"Mère, Mère."* "Where," he would ask, "is the horse?"

Eleven years before the Civil War, seventeen-year-old Joseph Brandenstein, later to become my Grandpa Joe, left his village of Humme, Germany, to seek gold in California, and also to avoid military conscription in the fatherland. He belonged to the popular Horatio Alger legend of that era. Only he didn't arrive in tatters, nor did he discover gold. Instead he was robbed of the tidy sum he'd brought along by some other pioneers. This bad luck turned into the good luck that was to make his fortunes. He left the mines and came to San Francisco. By 1861, after a round of jobs, he had saved enough money to open a tobacco shop. His timing was right. During the war Virginia tobacco was scarce, and Pa, who'd stocked up on it, suddenly found himself with the gold that had eluded him.

During a business trip to Philadelphia, he met and married a plump *gemütlichkeit* young woman named Kann, who as a child had left Germany's Westphalia to live with a cousin in Philadelphia.

I don't recall her first name. She was known to us as Ma. What I do remember is a story about her last name, Kann, which was given to her grandfather by Napoleonic tribunal. Until 1812, no Jewish family was permitted a surname. When her grandfather, nervous and trembling, appeared before the judge and was asked to choose a name, he stuttered, *"Ich kann—Ich kann nicht* [I cannot] —" The impatient judge snapped, "Very well, your name is Kann."

By the early 1870s, Pa Brandenstein was a leading member of the German merchant group to which belonged the influential citizens of San Francisco. Accordingly, he built himself a turreted Victorian mansion on the corner of Gough and California streets. (A yellow-brick apartment building stands there today.) But then, after pushing through the iron gate of the picket fence at the bottom, one had to climb a flight of wooden steps that led to a lawn bordered with concrete. Here began the final ascent of sandstone steps that glittered with mica and led to the oak door and its brass knocker —the entrance to Grandpa Joe Brandenstein's home. Mannie spent his childhood in this Victorian monster, where the overstuffed furniture, the cabinets filled with Liechtenstein beer mugs, and the whatnots barely left space in the parlor for the ladies in bustles to enjoy a cup of tea while they listened to young Mannie's comic imitations.

The house bulged on the exterior as well as the interior, for eventually there were eleven children. Pa isolated himself from the hubbub by retiring to the glass solarium, where he chewed on a cigar while he read German classics. Ma, left to cope with the youngsters, was never too busy to pat a child or laugh at one of Mannie's jokes.

Sometimes Ma sat at her bay window and peered through the lace curtains at the other grand homes on the street. But none was grander, she told herself, than the one Pa had built for her. In the courtyard below was her carriage house, and above it quarters for her coachman. Pa had presented her with a pair of matched roans, knowing that his unpretentious wife had a streak of sporting blood. She enjoyed going to the races almost as much as telling, now and then, a racy story remembered from her Westphalian childhood. In his way Pa spoiled her, and if at times he sneaked out to climb the back stairs of the Old Poodle Dog restaurant (now on Post Street, still popular, but minus the back stairs) or to enter the side door of Blanco's with a veiled and ostrich-plumed lady, he need not have gone to the trouble of secrecy. Ma willingly closed her eyes. Not that she evaded life. She accepted it.

Next to the Brandenstein mansion, and sharing a carriage entrance, lived Charles and Mike de Young, publishers of the *San Francisco Chronicle*. It was the era of yellow journalism, when few bothered to seek legal redress for defamation by the press. Action was far swifter and more direct. In 1881 Charles de Young was shot by the son of Kalloch, then a candidate for political office, in revenge for maligning his father. De Young died in his office at the *Chronicle*. Mike, now the sole publisher, was also shot, by another son in revenge for another father. It was over an accusation in the newspaper charging Claus Spreckels, head of the Hawaiian Sugar Company, with a stock swindle.

Standing by a bay window, Mannie, aged thirteen, saw Mr. de Young, bleeding profusely, being lifted out of a carriage and into his home.

"Ma," he screamed, "Mr. de Young is gushing blood all over the steps. He's dying, I'll bet he's dying!"

Ma, after a quick glance out the window, ordered Mannie to stop yelling. She walked over to the linen closet, took down some of her fine sheets, and tore them into strips. Handing them to Mannie she said, "Run next door and give these to Mrs. de Young for the wounds. *Mach schnell.*"

That Mike de Young managed to survive, Mannie attributed to the speed with which he bounded up the steps to deliver Ma's sheets.

As the years passed, the Brandenstein household grew quieter. Not because of less turmoil, but gradually each of the sisters and brothers married. Except Mannie and A. J. But then no one expected A. J. to marry. He was the smallest and most cautious of the brothers. He had a lavender-colored

Marmon car. He also had a mistress named Violet, no doubt chosen to match his car. He kept them both in storage. Mannie had a mistress too. Her name was business.

For his thirty-third birthday, the family and the in-laws gathered in the oak-paneled dining room, where the table was laden with fare to compete with the Hofbrau restaurant. The mahogany table needed its massive strength so as not to cave in under its burden of dill pickles, smoked salmon, herring, homemade jams, and, for dessert, *Lebkuchen*, a layered chocolate torte crowned with candles. But none to grow on.

"You'll never be a giant, my son," Ma said, when the rest had left the room. "Still you're a big man. When," she asked, looking at his slightly balding head, "will you bring me home another daughter?"

Mannie put his arms around the waist he could not fully encompass. "You'll always be my girl."

"Don't *Schmeichel* me with flattery. Pa says you've been doing fine selling coffee. Maybe you and your brother Max will go into partnership. It's time," she said patting the few strands on his head, "you found a wife. I notice Greta Haas has grown very pretty. Her mother," she added, "comes from my village in Germany."

Mannie placed a kiss on Ma's plump cheek, but his mind was on a different scene. In Golden Gate Park, there was a girl sitting sedately on a bench beside a heavy-set woman leaning on a French parasol. The young woman was statuesque and reserved, so unlike his tiny animated sisters. Mannie, driving by in the Brandenstein carriage, was tipping his bowler to the girl.

Less than twenty blocks away from the Brandenstein home on the hill of California Street was another house, built on the leveled sand dunes near the panhandle of Golden Gate Park. It was a slimly elegant structure with marble entrance steps, and next to its bulging Victorian neighbors it seemed like an undernourished child overpowered by fat matrons. (The building still stands, transformed once into a funeral parlor and later into a Buddhist temple.) The home belonged to my Alsatian grandparents, Daniel and Julie Roth. It was here, where the parquet floors and the Louis Quinze furniture were kept at a polished gloss, that Renée and her elder sister grew up.

Their upbringing reflected the austerity of the exterior of their home, although my genial Bon-papa Roth might have wished it otherwise. Apart from a game of billiards and his cigars, whose ashes Julie cleaned up immediately, he had few forms of relaxation. Yet, he was proud of his intelligent wife and of himself for having fulfilled a promise he'd made long ago to the serious girl from his neighboring village in Alsace. As soon as he made his fortune in *Les Etats-Unis*—and he never doubted that would be soon—he would send for her.

Like Pa Brandenstein, Daniel Roth came to San Francisco in the early 1850s, from the village of Bouxvillaire, Alsace. As a boy he had admired Julie, who lived nearby in the village of Neuxvillaire. She was forever reading books and doing fine hand embroideries from her own designs. Her intense eyes, bright as though some light burned behind them, seemed to wait for something beyond the rolling hills of the countryside.

He was eighteen when he came down the gangplank of the French freighter that docked at New Orleans. Dan Roth had twenty dollars in gold Louis in his pocket, a passport signed by Napoleon III in his portmanteau, and some imitation jewelry packed between his clothes in a satchel. Filled with the confidence of youth, he was sure that before long he would be able to send for his Julie.

After spending weeks peddling cameo brooches and cheap jewelry from door to door, and using up his Louis for meager board and bed, he decided he must push on to the West, and there he would find gold.

Seven more years, and like Jacob, he'd not realized his dream. He'd worked in the woolen mills of Oregon and the gold mines of California before he finally arrived by muleback in San Francisco. Daniel took the first job he could find—a smelly noisy one at that—driving hogs along the then dirt road of what was to become San Francisco's finest avenue, Van Ness. Like the Pied Piper, a horde of children followed him to his destination, the slaughterhouse called Butchertown, where the odors from the *abattoir* mingled with those from the sluggish waters of Islais Creek. But the children did not dance to the tune of a flute; they jeered and taunted and imitated the squeals of the frightened animals.

Yet, like it or not, he was in the right business. San Franciscans who'd struck it rich were literally living "high off the hog." Soon Daniel was made manager of the packing plant and he could at last keep his promise to Julie. From his mother he learned that Julie, an orphan now, had gone to Paris to live with an aunt. But how was he to approach her? He suddenly thought of a plan. At the City of Paris, one of San Francisco's smartest shops in the sixties, he bought a fine paisley shawl. In its folds he discreetly enclosed a passage ticket. Three months later, having sailed around the Horn, Julie arrived in San Francisco harbor. Daniel was at the docks. Around her shoulders was the shawl, and as she pushed back the veil from her bonnet, he could see the glow in her eyes.

The distance between the overstuffed mansion on California and the slim *maison* of the Roth's near Golden Gate Park could not be measured by blocks alone. Nor was the chasm caused by religion. Both families belonged to the Jewish faith. The well-to-do Germans attended Temple Emanu-El; the French elite worshipped at Beth Israel. It was nationality that kept them apart. The old enmity between French and German was an open wound kept festering by the recent loss of Alsace to the Germans in the Franco-Prussian War.

When social obligations forced Julie and Ma to meet, the two would exchange polite formal greetings.

Only once had they met on what might have been more intimate terms. It turned out to be an unfortunate encounter. On one weekend the Brandenstein's private carriage and the Roth's hired one arrived at Aetna Springs resort, one after another. Ma, busy with her baggage, did not see Julie. In the dining room that evening the two were seated far apart, and it was not until the next morning that they passed one another on the circular stairway. Julie smiled a good morning. Ma nodded, averting her head. The snub bit deep into Julie. And if it annoyed Julie to have to include Mannie at Renée's debut ball, it annoyed her even more to watch her daughter dancing away half the evening in Mannie's arms. Nor did she fail to notice that on Sundays when Renée accompanied her to Golden Gate Park, Renée invariably chose a bench close to the driveway. Though Julie made no mention of this, she knew that Renée, while dutifully reading out loud from Stendahl or an article in *Paris Soir*, waited for the moment when the Brandenstein brougham, filled with laughing brothers and sisters, would come rolling along the red rock drive. As if on a current of understanding, Renée would look up at the right instant to see Mannie tip his derby in gay salute. Julie tapped her parasol. No. This would not do. Renée, like any other *comme-il-faut jeune fille*, must make a suitable match with a young man of the same background. And although Julie could stop their Sunday walks to Golden Gate Park, she could not prevent Renée from meeting Mannie at balls, the holiday parties at the Cliff House, all-day excursions to the beach on horse-drawn streetcars, and other social events of the season. Determined to have her own way, Julie suggested to Daniel that they take Renée on a trip to Paris. To her surprise, her usually obliging husband refused. Yet, if Julie was determined, so was her daughter. Finally, Renée confessed to Maman that if she could not marry Manfred, she would marry no one.

Only because Renée was so persistent about what Maman called an *infatuation obstinée* was she at last permitted to invite Manfred to call after dinner. As Maman explained, to share a meal with a German was unthinkable. Nevertheless, she made a bargain with her daughter. She would observe the young man, and if she approved she would give Renée a signal. The sign was a handkerchief. If Maman dropped it, that meant yes. If she kept it in her hand it would mean no.

In a parlor, whose cream-colored walls and crystal sconces shed a mellow glow, two men and two women sat sipping after-dinner coffee. As the older man set down his demitasse on a marble-top table to take out his cigar cutter, the balding young man with the moustache followed suit.

"How about trying one of mine, Mr. Roth?" The younger man extended a pin-seal case and flipped it open.

"Manfred," protested the young woman with the exquisite straight brows, "I thought you only smoked cigarettes."

Mannie laughed. "Caught in the act of trying to bribe your father with a Corona Corona."

Dan Roth selected a cigar, crackled it next to his ear, then bent to sniff it. "Can tell this is choice tobacco," he said, snipping off the end.

For the first time the older woman looked up from her coffee cup. "If you ask me, the price men pay for their cigars nowadays is ridiculous." Her stiff taffeta skirt rustled as if underscoring her annoyance.

Before Julie's frown could set in a crease, Mannie leaned toward her. "Madame Roth," he said, "may I compliment you on your coffee. It has an unusual flavor. Perhaps you would let me in on the secret of your blend."

"Monsieur Mannie—Monsieur Brandenstein," Julie said, correcting herself, "from one in the coffee business this is indeed a *beau* compliment."

Almost flirtatiously she lifted her lace-trimmed handkerchief to her broad, well-shaped nose. Renée watched the

fragile bit of cambric in Maman's hand as though it were a
heavy flag about to drop of its own weight. Maman avoided
her eyes. Instead she listened to Manfred, who had begun a
discussion of the meaning of words. "Madame Roth," he
asked, "do you know the origin of 'sincere'?"

"Of course. It comes from the Greek *sine cire*, without
wax."

The curve of Julie's lips gave no indication of whether
she was pleased or annoyed at the question.

Manfred beamed. "Very few people know that."

What was the matter with Manfred? Was he trying to
judge Maman instead of her judging him?

As Maman went on to explain how certain Greek sculp-
tors used wax to cover flaws in their works, Papa blew smoke
rings toward the ceiling.

Julie rose from her chair and brushed aside a puff of
smoke with her handkerchief. "Daniel, I'm sure you would
enjoy a game of billiards with Monsieur Brandenstein, while
Renée watches. Now, if you will excuse me, I am going to my
room. I'll join you later."

In the downstairs game room, Renée sat on a carved
Italian chair. Her eyes absently followed the players while her
thoughts remained fixed on Maman upstairs. Dared she hope
that Manfred had managed to break through Maman's de-
fenses? And if so, would Maman harden herself again with
the reminder that he was the son of Germans, the son of a
plain little woman who once had snubbed her? With an effort,
Renée forced her attention back to the players. The game was
nearly over. Suddenly she heard Papa say, "A setup for a
three-cushion shot. I'm as good as beaten."

Manfred laughed. "I don't know about that." He circled
the table, knelt below the baize, studied the balls, and, without chalking his cue, took aim. The cue slipped off the ball.
"Your game," Manfred said, and went over to shake Papa's
hand.

Papa looked dubious. "Didn't you forget to chalk your cue?"

"I couldn't have. No, I have no alibi, other than I lost to a better player."

Neither man seemed to have noticed the click of Maman's French heels against the hardwood steps. As Maman came into the room, Renée bit into her lips as if surface pain could ward off a far deeper one.

"I see you have finished your game. *Bonsoir*, Monsieur Brandenstein." Maman's voice was formal and she did not extend her hand.

"Thank you for your hospitality." Manfred smiled, ignoring Maman's coolness. "Before I leave I would like to tell you how much my mother admires you."

Julie's answering smile was brittle and she started toward the staircase. Manfred seemed to grasp the empty air after her.

"Wait!" he said. "I know Ma would never forgive me for talking out of turn, but I've got to say it. Remember the time she met you at Aetna Springs. Poor Ma had just dropped her teeth down —" He paused, and went on. "Let's call it the wash basin. Anyway, they floated away." Now Manfred was laughing. "Imagine my ma not being able to greet you with her regular smile!"

Renée gasped. How could Manfred mention anything so vulgar! For a moment there was silence, and then Maman said in a voice without inflection, "Monsieur Brandenstein, you are indeed what the Greeks call sincere."

She started up the first step. Then the second. "*Mon Dieu*, Renée," she said, "how careless of me! I dropped my handkerchief!"

Their wedding was a grand affair, held at high noon in the Crystal Ballroom of the Palace Hotel. The year was 1899. The newspapers reported it as the union of two prominent San Francisco families, descendants of California pioneers.

There were detailed descriptions of the bride, a ravishing brunette whose real Alençon veil cascaded like foam on the ruby red runway, and of the sartorial taste of the groom, a promising young coffee merchant. No mention was made that the groom stood at the altar a head shorter than the bride.

The guests waited in silence as the rabbi offered the goblet of wine first to Renée and then to Mannie, and intoned the words, "This is the cup of life, symbolizing joy and experience you will share. . . . As a rabbi and according to the law of California, I now pronounce you man and wife." No sooner were these words spoken than Mannie gave Renée a sedate public kiss and the festivities began.

Ordinarily, Daniel and Julie Roth were cautious with their money, but for this occasion they untied their purse strings. Although the French had been forced to surrender to the enemy, they could not be forced from style and graciousness.

When the music paused, the laughter and chatter around the horseshoe bridal table was punctuated by the pop of champagne corks. The individual gilt-inscribed menus rested in ivory holders and overflowed with names to confound the Germans: *truite bleu, champignons sous cloche, bombe à la Napoléon.* That the chef of the Palace was a Parisian was a little secret victory for Julie Roth.

The French relatives raised their glasses to the bride and groom with the toast, *"A votre santé!"* The Germans retaliated with, *"Hoch Soll zehr Leben!"*

When it was finally over, the wedding guests gathered in the Palace court while the hotel guests leaned over their balconies to watch the beautiful young woman in the form-fitting tailored suit being assisted into a private carriage by the young man with a bowler that didn't quite sit at ease on his head. The spectacle took place in the courtyard of the hotel, which has since been enclosed to become the Garden Court dining room of the Sheraton-Palace. While its elegance remains, it is not as impressive as on the day when cries of *"Bonne chance, Renée"* and *"Glück, Mannie!"* rose to the balconies as the newlyweds were pelted with a shower of rice. The liveried coachman clucked to the horses and smartly snapped the reins as the carriage wheeled into Montgomery Street. Wedding guests viewed the departing couple being escorted by a fat pink cupid with golden bow and arrow painted on the back of the carriage hood.

There were two handkerchiefs this time: one in Ma Brandenstein's plump hand, the other in Julie's capable fingers. Neither dropped them from their eyes until the sound of the hooves had faded away.

Once inside the carriage, Mannie removed his bowler, adjusted his toupee, and gave Renée a warm private kiss. The toupee was Renée's idea. "Darling," she suggested before their wedding, "I think you should wear a toupee." Mannie, much in love, agreed. "And," Renée added, "it would be more dignified if you were called Manfred instead of Mannie."

Dad, who had been known as Mannie all his life, was a little bewildered by these requests, but once more said, "Yes, dear."

So Mannie became Manfred and covered the few strands, which crossed his head in narrow gauge tracks, with a hairpiece. Now he clung to his toupee all the way from the altar, to the ferryboat ride to Oakland mole where the wind threatened to blow it off, and onto the train that was to take him and his bride on a honeymoon tour of the Rockies. Their wedding night was to be spent in Sacramento. Mannie was as insistent about that as Renée about his changed personality. He wanted to check coffee sales at the grocery stores the next morning.

Aboard the train he settled his bride in the chair car, then sank into the seat next to her. Outside the tidelands stretched in a gray sheath. The porter came through with his taper to light the gas lamps. The hiss of the gas and the rhythmic click of train wheels, combined with the champagne bubbles dancing in his head, made him sleepy. He nodded against the red plush and soon was snoring gently. Renée, handsome in her new beige suit with the lace jabot, sat erect, a little wounded by Manfred's quick escape. She plucked at two grains of rice caught in the veil of her sailor.

Passengers smiled at the obvious newlyweds. All at once, the discreet smiles turned to open laughter. Under lowered lashes Renée studied the passengers. They were no longer admiring her but watching the groom. The train's jouncing had dislodged his toupee. It had begun to rise in the air, like the Indian rope trick.

Pink faced, she nudged him. "Manfred, Manfred. Wake up!"

He came to, with a start. The toupee fell to the floor and bounced along the aisle. He leaned to retrieve it and, as he did so, caught sight of his shiny scalp in the sliver of mirror between the car windows. He waved a hand at the familiar reflection. "Hello, Mannie," he said chuckling. "Good-bye, Manfred."

My father never wore a toupee again. And no one ever called him Manfred. Except Renée.

III

THE PORTRAIT

*I*N THE beginning I believed my father created coffee. Later I thought he started the MJB Company. This was not true either. It was my Uncle Max, Mannie's oldest brother, importer of tea and rice from the Orient, who founded the business. When Mannie joined the firm in 1899, he did so on one condition, that coffee be added. As he told me, he was in coffee from the "grounds up."

His first business venture at the age of twenty-one was a small wholesale grocery that dealt in a variety of products from coffee to ketchup. Enthusiastic about a ketchup bottle with a new sealproof cap, he demonstrated it to a prospective customer by waving the bottle in midair. The no-blow cap flew off, and ketchup spilled all over the customer's suit and red-streaked Mannie's prematurely balding head. Not only did he lose a sale but he also had to pay the customer's cleaning bill.

Head ketchuppy but unbowed, Mannie decided to concentrate on coffee. In the days before sex became a conversation piece, he advertised his brand with a colored poster that featured a young lady reclining in bed. In her hand she held her morning cup of coffee, and a contented smile was on her rosebud mouth. In large letters blazed the word, CLIMAX.

With second thoughts, he next put out a tin that displayed a sleeping Turk. This blend was called MUST-AV-IT. After he became his brother Max's partner, Mannie put the snoozing Turk to sleep permanently. He renamed the coffee after Max's initials, MJB, followed by the word WHY? The brand was known as MJB COFFEE WHY?

As soon as I was old enough to smell the coffee, I asked my father, "Why the WHY?" With a twinkle he answered, "What's the difference, as long as people ask. That makes sales."

I had begun to gather bits and pieces of his philosophy but was unsure how to put them together. It was like trying to understand what happened after the 1906 earthquake. I heard my parents talk about San Francisco unified by disaster —words too complicated for me to grasp. I knew that my French grandparents and my German ones helped us each in their own way. The Roths, traveling in Europe, read incorrect scare headlines, "San Francisco Under Water (instead of "Out of Water") . . . Thousands Perish in Flames." Immediately they booked return passage and rented a home in Berkeley, where we all lived together for the next two years. Pa Brandenstein, alone after Ma died, set up temporary business offices for his sons in his house on California Street with a temporary warehouse at Spear and Mission streets.

Mannie commuted each day by ferryboat to Pa's home. It was on a morning ride that he overheard some preachers discussing the punishment God had visited on San Francisco for its evil ways, which I gathered had something to do with the Barbary Coast—a part of the coastline no one had ever pointed out to me. While the sea gulls wheeled and screeched overhead, a gentleman seated on a bench next to Dad pulled out a note pad and pencil and began writing. With a glance at the preachers and a sly smile at Mannie, he tore off the sheet and handed it to him. On it were jotted the lines: "If as they say, God spanked the town for being over frisky, why did he burn the churches down and save Hotalings Whiskey?" Dad chuckled and the man introduced himself as Charles Field. He was, Mannie realized, the editor of the old *Sunset* magazine and the brother of Eugene Field, famed poet of "Wynken', Blynken', and Nod."

Stories like these, Mannie was fond of repeating. He seldom mentioned the work, faith, and bounce it took to rebuild his business. Since "Everybody was doing it," like the turkey trot, I suppose he took his part for granted. And I, as a child, took for granted his announcement one evening in Berkeley. "Renée, I have a surprise for you." Before she could question him, he snapped his fingers. "Trois bleu, boom, boom, I've rented a home in San Francisco, on Pacific Avenue."

Our exile was over! Mother wept with happiness. She could resume the cosmopolitan life; Mannie could concentrate on the WHY? in coffee without having to commute to Berkeley; while I, regardless of where we lived, pursued the enigma of my brother Joe.

There was one thing I couldn't forgive my brother. He was four years older than myself. He told me I was found on a doorstep in a clothes basket and adopted out of pity. My real name was not Ruth Brandenstein, but Rabinowitz Finkelstein. This, he warned, was a dark secret, never to be mentioned to anyone, particularly to Renée and Mannie. If I brought home a poor report card, he would say, "What can you expect, Rabbie? Your real folks were probably morons."

Could he be right? Was that why Dad's nickname for me was Peanuts. He said he liked the name because it reminded him of the butcher boys at the ball park who yelled, "Peanuts, popcorn, French mixed candy." And was that why mother called me *Chérie*? Were they avoiding my real name?

I stretched like a rubber band between jealousy and admiration for my brother. My jealousy focused on an oil portrait of Joe that hung over Renée's Italian commode under an orange light, as if destined to glow perpetually. He wore a sailor suit with a whistle dangling from his blouse. The only picture my mother had of me was a photograph taken at the age of two holding a sand pail, a bow in my frizzy hair, and my mouth open in adenoidal surprise. It hung on the back of her dressing-room door.

If I had mixed emotions about Joe, I had none about Renée and Mannie. She was a mother to be admired, worshipped from afar, beautiful as I could never be. It shocked me that she wanted me to call her my pal. Mannie was the one who could laugh with me, who would teach me the secrets of life.

Released from the restrictions of the crowded living conditions in Berkeley to the spacious comfort of the house on Pacific Avenue, Renée reverted to her desire for perfection in her home. Early in her marriage she had told my father, "Mannie, you run your business. I'll run my home." Mannie agreed, saying with a chuckle, "Who'll run for the streetcar?"

Nonetheless, he left Renée a free hand. She was convinced that people, like butter, could be pressed into a mold. Especially our maids. This belief produced an endless parade of maids, all of whom were French. One morning a newly hired girl, not yet introduced to Mannie, rapped on the bedroom door to bring in the breakfast tray.

Mannie dived beneath the covers, leaving only a small expanse of pink dome to peep above the top sheet.

"Ah!" the French maid exclaimed delightedly, "*Madame a un bébé. I did not know Madame had a bébé.*"

Mannie flung back the covers to reveal his full-blown moustache. He winked. The astonished girl dropped the tray, smashing Renée's Limoges china while the coffee pot spilled its contents onto the Brussels carpet.

The next morning there was a new French maid.

According to mother, home and business did not mix, but travel was something we should all share. She thought of travel as a cultural pursuit and renewed an old campaign for a trip to Europe. By Europe she meant Paris. Mannie thought of travel in terms of checking coffee sales in the United States and visiting grocery stores. Sometimes, carrying a suitcase in each hand, he would parade around Renée in the living room and chant, "I'm going traveling, I'm going traveling." Yet he was unable to resist her.

One day in June, the five of us—Mother, Dad, Joe, and myself and Henriette—set out for Europe. Henriette was the French governess who was to supervise the children's culture. She was pretty, with dark bangs above sparkly eyes. I hated her. She adored Joe.

On board ship Joe and Henriette played shuffleboard. At least she pretended to play while she eyed the ship's officers. Joe kept me informed of her score, which was higher with the officers than with the game. Mother tramped the deck in a divided khaki skirt as if trying to stamp out a brush fire. Mannie, who hated fresh air, except at a ball park or a prizefight, passed the time in the smoking room playing poker. Left alone in the cabin, I whoopsed in seasick revenge.

Once we were installed at the Hôtel Continentale in Paris, Mannie and Renée followed their natural bent. Mother spent her time at places of *haute couture*, Paquin or Moly-neux. Dad followed his hobby. He visited every *épicerie* in Paris and was horrified to find that the French housewife was buying green coffee and roasting it at home in an iron frying pan.

In the evenings he would take Renée to theater, suggesting the Folies Bergères or the Comédie Française. When Renée countered, "I would prefer the opera," he muttered, "When I say needles, you say pins." During the day while Renée shopped, he often occupied himself visiting Cook and Sons, where he could find other Americans. But no matter where he went he took taxis. That left Joe and me and Henriette. We could no longer count on Henriette. According to Joe she was now making "goo-goo" eyes at the manager of the hotel, whose pointed waxed moustache matched his pointed shiny shoes. One afternoon she shooed us off and entrusted Joe to take me through the Louvre. On the way I saw a *nou-nou* in the park nursing a baby. One breast was exposed and I asked my brother what she was doing. In disgust he answered, "Don't you know anything about nature, Rabbie? She's giving the baby milk." To which I asked, looking at the one covered breast, "Does mush come out of the other side?"

Anxious to get rid of me, Joe rushed me through the Louvre, but not fast enough for me not to stand in awe of all the portraits. Just like Joe's over Mother's commode.

Back in the hotel once more, and bored with me, Joe decided to run through the floors from the fifteenth down to the lobby ringing the fire alarm. All the guests rushed out. The fire engines arrived and there were shouts of *"Feux, feux!"*

In the midst of the excitement, Henriette came out of the manager's office buttoning her blouse, while he buttoned his frock coat.

When the hubbub subsided, Mannie burst into our room. Renée started to explain what had happened, but he interrupted with, "Those cabdrivers are a bunch of *coochons!*"

"Cochon," Renée corrected, wincing at the mutilation of the language.

"So, *coochon* or *cochon*, they're *goniffs*." He went on to splutter about a cabdriver who had taken him to the Right Bank, then the Left Bank and all but into the Seine when he'd told him to drive to Cook's.

Not until later was she able to tell Dad about the fire. Who, she wondered, had put in a false alarm? Where was Henriette? Wasn't she with the children? That's when Henriette turned into what Joe called a female Benedict Arnold. She claimed she had a headache and was lying down when she saw Joe running down the halls pulling fire cords. She tried to run after him but too late.

The decision was made, then and there. Joe was banished to a Prussian boarding school. Pale faced, he packed his bag. I had visions of his ears being pulled to the ground by a schoolmaster if he didn't mind. Suddenly I loved my brother. But what to do about it? I was alone with the traitor, Henriette. I begged for drawing lessons in a desire to create a self-portrait like the ones I'd seen at the Louvre—one to vie with Joe's.

Mother was delighted, and Mannie announced one morning that a Madame Kachoo, or something that sounded like a sneeze, would be coming at eleven to give me a lesson.

At the appointed hour Renée presented Madame, a crow of a woman, who looked too dried up to sneeze. Under her arm she held a big white pad. In one hand she clutched the worn strings of a sagging mesh bag. She placed the pad on a desk, pulled out some colored crayons from the bag, and turning to me, ran a yellow paw over my head. "What curls—*comme un mouton.*"

She seemed to think telling me my hair was like lamb's wool was a great compliment. Already my first joy had vanished. So had Mother, who, before shutting the door, had promised to return in a little while with Dad.

Within minutes Madame Sneeze discovered her pupil had not a glimmer of talent, a fact she met equably while she fixed her attention on my hardly touched breakfast tray. She picked up the cover of a dish and, with the pecking motions of a bird, demolished the croissants, then licked a finger into the strawberry *comfiture*, only pausing to remark that to be an *artiste* was to be hungry. Not bothering to wipe her finger, she told me she would show me how to draw a perfect picture of a big "doggee." She clamped her sticky hand over my moist fist and produced a greyhound that fairly raced across the page. Renée and Manfred chose that moment to enter the room.

"*Tiens!*" Madame exclaimed. "*Vraiment beaucoup de talent.*"

Mannie interrupted this flow of French with, "*Trois bleu, boom, boom.*" Madame Sneeze held out her hand and asked, "What time would you like me to give *la petite* another lesson?" and added with a sharp look at Mannie, "That will be five dollars for today."

Mannie put the money into her extended claw. "Mrs. Brandenstein will telephone you for another appointment," he said, and showed her to the door.

Mother was admiring my work. "I never thought you could draw. I can't believe it. We should have given you lessons long ago. Manfred, come here. Look at what your daughter has done."

Mannie hardly glanced at the picture. His eyes were fixed on mine.

"Did you do this all alone, Peanuts?" he asked.

At first I only nodded, but once the nod had bobbed up and down a couple of times, I backed it up with a tremulous "yes"; and after the first uncertainty in my voice, I became emphatic. "Yes, yes—all alone."

"I can't believe it," Renée repeated.

"Why, that's wonderful," Mannie said, and his eyes were not smiling. "Since you drew that picture once, it will be easy for you to make another."

"Now?"

It was Mannie's turn to nod.

I was dumbfounded. "I'm awfully tired—"

"That's all right," Mannie interrupted. "You may have all of one hour to draw me another dog."

Without giving me a chance to make an excuse, he and Renée left me alone with the drawing pad. Mannie had asked me for another dog. He couldn't have given a better name for what I produced. I was crying when, head bent, I handed my creation to him.

He said nothing for what seemed a long time. Then he put a hand under my lowered chin.

"Maybe, Peanuts, you haven't learned to draw. But you have learned a very important lesson."

He could be a gently stern parent. I suffered a long time and hardly paid attention to Mannie's translation of a letter just received from Joe. It was postmarked Wiesbaden. There were long descriptions about *Tannenbaum* forests and the frosty nights. It wasn't until Mannie read Joe's final words about how wonderful boarding school was and how much he was learning that I noticed a gloom like mine had settled over the others. What was wrong? Henriette had gone for her handkerchief and Renée lifted her neck as if the collar of her blouse was choking her.

Mannie folded the letter and jammed it back into the envelope.

"Renée," he said, "phone the concierge and tell him to get me a cab. I'm going over to Cook's. They can have Joe meet us at Le Havre next Thursday."

"Yes, Renée dear," he went on in reply to the question in Mother's eyes. "That's the day the *Aquitania* sails to New York."

Everyone smiled again. That is, all but me. It was great to go home, but what was to happen to my acquisition of culture?

On the Wednesday before we left for Le Havre and while Henriette packed, Renée shampooed my hair in the tile basin. It was a tiresome proceeding and I was sent out to the balcony of our room to dry my curly mop in the sun. Through eyes like dormer windows in a thatched roof, I peered at the passers-by: the aged woman with half a yard of bread under her arm, the elderly man whose black felt hat was turning a little green, a *cheminot* in a baggy blue blouse, two lovers hand in hand. Somebody was whistling at me and I leaned over the iron rail and said boldly, "Are you talking to me?"

It was a young man, with yellow straw hat tilted back from his eyes. He blew me a kiss and said, "*Certainement, chérie!* What be-ootiful hair!" He loosed a strap from his arm and pulled out the accordian pleats of a camera. "I take your picture and put it all over Paris—all over France!"

"Like MJB COFFEE WHY?"

He shrugged. "I do not know what you mean by coffee why? I want you for a *modèle, bébé*. An advertisement for the Jolie Hair Tonic."

While he squinted into his ancient camera I began to tell him about Mannie's ad and the question mark and when I paused, he waved his arms to get me to pose. "Mysterious, eh? Now *bébé*, please let me have a nice smile."

About six weeks after we arrived back in San Francisco, Renée received an inlaid ivory cigarette box she had purchased at the Paris flea market. It was packaged in excelsior and protected with newspapers. We all sat around to admire her bargain, and as she unwrapped the last piece of *Paris Soir*, my portrait came to light. It was a large ad showing a mop of hair with a big question mark above and a bottle of Jolie Hair Tonic below. I recognized the picture immediately.

"That's me," I said, trying to remain calm.

My brother Joe gave a hoot. "Who the heck would know who posed for that picture? It could be anybody."

It was true. My hair was hanging over my face. But I had made my mark on Paris after all!

"What does 'power-quee' mean?" Mannie asked, looking at the word next to the question mark.

"It's French for 'why,' " Renée told him.

Mannie rubbed the corner of his moustache. "How do you suppose a hair tonic concern in Paris got hold of the idea from my ad? It's quite a compliment. But how?"

I told them. While waiting for the cameraman to focus, to get me to pose properly, I had given away the trade secrets of MJB. I had told that young man what Mannie had told me. "It doesn't matter what you ask so long as you ask."

Joe whistled, just like the photographer. "So that's really you Ruth, my sister."

"Not bad, Peanuts," Mannie said. "Maybe I should make you a junior partner."

IV

A DAY
AT THE OFFICE

"*PEANUTS,*" *DAD* asked me one morning at breakfast, "how would you like to come to my office?"

I nodded my excitement. "Without Joe?"

"Just the two of us. Want you to learn the inside operations of MJB."

He pushed aside the newspaper with his favorite columnist, KCB, and finished his boiled egg with bacon bits, while I rushed for my coat. Dad really meant it. I was his junior partner.

Outside, the black Packard Landolet, his latest gift to Renée, which looked like a hearse to me, waited at the curb. So did our new chauffeur, Carter, in uniform and puttees. He'd been with us two weeks, which qualified him as an old retainer.

I climbed into the back seat and leaned against the striped upholstery. We raced down Pacific Avenue and ignored the indignant clang of the dinky cable car bell. Up the steep California Street hills he double kicked the clutch with a smoothness I aimed to imitate some day. We cut down Kearny across Market to skid row, where all the men seemed to shuffle. I caught a glimpse of one man lying asleep in a doorway, his soiled hat in the gutter. He looked up for a moment at the barreling black car and spit some red juice in our direction. Poor man, I thought. He must have consumption, like my Aunt Jeanne.

Carter pushed a thumb against the horn, which responded ooh, ah!, ooh, ah!, and a little mongrel jumped, just in time, from under the front wheels. All this seemed to me like the large asbestos curtain at the Orpheum Theatre with its painted ads—part of a show about to begin. Now the streets widened and the rumbling trucks, their exhaust pipes popping, swerved between the car tracks on Mission. We came close to hitting the cab of a truck whose driver sat at the wheel, shirt sleeves rolled up showing a muscular, hairy arm. Big and powerful I thought. Maybe I'd marry a truck driver some day. Or perhaps I would settle for Taro, our Japanese butler, with jet hair and mysterious smile. Then I forgot my future plans in the excitement of the moment. Already I could see the freight trains in the Southern Pacific yards. And in the distance towered a big wooden coffee pot with the letters "MJB WHY?"

Carter braked the car to a stop. I jumped out and pushed through the entrance door. Immediately I was catapulted into a sea of wonderful odors—a mixture of roasted coffee, pungent tea, and machine oil.

Once inside Mannie's office, he left me with a promise to return in a little while. I glanced around, then went over and sat down in the leather chair behind his rolltop desk. A student lamp with a green glass shade cast a theatrical glow, so that the brass cuspidor, within easy reach, glinted in irregular tones. The spindle on top of the desk looked like a stiletto impaling mounds of inked accounts. Against the wall the big black safe, gilt letters peeling a little, announced M. J. Brandenstein Company, Importers, Coffee, Tea, and Rice 1892. Above the leather couch, with the two loose buttons on the pillow pad, was an array of family photos. And right next to an old-fashioned red coffee grinder was a photograph of a beautiful dark-haired lady in a Spanish costume, a long necklace cascading onto her overripe bosom. It was signed "To dear Mannie, from Mabel." There was one more picture—a tinted chrome of a powerful Negro dancing inside a roped square with small gloves on his big fists, and an inscription on the American flag in the corner, "To Mannie, the Sport . . . Jack Johnson, Reno, July 4th, 1910."

I watched the pendulum of the wall clock with the black Roman numerals tick away the minutes. There was no other sound in the room.

I tiptoed to the door, opened it, and peeked out. From where I stood I could see the huge revolving table at the far end of the hall, a circle of tea tumblers on its top. Uncle Eddie was stooped over it picking up one after another of the steaming cups. He sucked in the tea with a gargling noise, held it in his mouth for an instant, and then spat an arc of amber liquid into an hourglass spittoon. Bull's-eye each time.

I turned and saw Uncle Charlie, Mannie's youngest brother, come out of a side office. He was struggling with a large carton. Uncle Charlie was blond, fuzzy haired and preferred shouting to using ordinary tones. He was a great one for patent medicines. When the cashier, a plump little lady he called Sweetie-Pie with legs that seemed to have no ankles, broke out with hives, which she did often when the brothers got too argumentative, Charlie would whip out some cream and smear it all over her face. Above her shrieks of protest he assured her this was a magic remedy that could cure anything, including the "epizoodics."

Now, he called, "Ruth, come here. I want to show you something."

As I approached he pulled a shiny black belt from the

carton. "Twenty-four of these," he announced. "By ordering twenty-four, I could get them wholesale. Trouble is I ordered brown ones."

Before I could say, "Sorry," he shouted, "Mr. Hartwick, Mr. Hartwick."

From a cubbyhole toward the rear, out popped a wiry short man with button features. "Don't yell, Charlie. I'm right here."

Mr. Hartwick was MJB's glorified errand boy. He drove the office car at breakneck speed in an effort to keep up with the brothers' conflicting missions. They always called him Mr. Hartwick, but he never addressed them by anything but their first names.

"Mr. Hartwick," Charlie said, his voice rising, "drive over to the Owl drugstore and get me the strongest dye remover you can find, and some brown shoe polish."

He fished two one-dollar bills from his pocket. Mr. Hartwick shook his head. "Have to pick up Max's wife and take her to Magnin's and drop Eddie's suitcase at his house and then—"

Uncle Charlie pressed an extra fifty cents into Mr. Hartwick's palm. "Get yourself a beer and bring the stuff back from the drugstore."

"OK, but cover for me if I'm late."

Charlie gave him a shove toward the front entrance.

About to turn back to Dad's office, he intercepted me in the hall. "Peanuts," he said, "I've got a conference. Sit down on the bench outside. It won't take long."

Since voices were never lowered, I could hear my father talking to Mr. Altman, the sales manager. Altman I had met before. He was my idea of a Prussian officer, and his stiff walk and preciseness made me shiver. When I told Dad about this he laughed. "Altman's OK. He fits the Gilbert and Sullivan lines, 'I've never yet made one mistake. I'd like to for variety's sake.'"

Now I heard Mannie say, "Altman, I'm sure all the buyers will choose MJB; it's that good."

"That's nonsense," Mr. Altman insisted. "There are as many different tastes in blends as there are buyers. With four buyers and four samples besides MJB, how can they all choose our brand?"

"Tell you what I'll do. I'll bet you a twenty-dollar gold piece that every buyer will choose MJB."

"You're on," Mr. Altman said, barely suppressing a snicker. "Let's go."

Mr. Altman marched out of the office while Mannie followed across the hall to the tasting table. I trailed behind, anxious to learn the secrets of the business. Dad saw me and, while he diverted the buyers' attention to packages on the shelf, he winked at me and pointed out the cup which contained MJB. And as quick as his wink, he poured some brownish liquid into that cup.

I watched each buyer lift a cup, rinse the brew in his mouth and spit it out into the brass spittoon. Each then noted a rating onto a card. Mannie could not resist a shout when he turned over the control cards and showed Mr. Altman the results. All four buyers had chosen MJB.

Mr. Altman's rigid features struggled between incredulity and pride. He reached into a pocket, brought out a twenty-dollar gold piece, and offered it to Mannie. Dad restrained him with a chuckle. "No bet, Mr. Altman."

"No bet? But we—"

"You don't owe me a cent. Just before the tasting I slipped a little whiskey into the MJB brew."

The buyers were laughing.

Mannie collected me as he and Uncle Max walked back to Dad's office. I sat down on the leather couch and played with a loose button and hardly listened till I heard Uncle Max, round and cozy as a sofa cushion, say in unusually stern tones, "Eddie thinks you're spending too much on coffee ads.

He's got a hunch we should be pushing rice. Thinks it's got a big future. Even greater than coffee or tea."

Mannie shrugged. "Could be. If rice is Eddie's new baby, he better remember mine's coffee. And it's no baby."

"I'm not going to argue with you, but—" Before Max could finish, he was interrupted by a crescendo of commotion coming from the hall. We all ran out the doorway and joined a crowd of stenographers and office workers around the tasting table. Uncle Eddie, who usually stood nearby, had disappeared. Uncle Charlie was shouting for smelling salts. In one hand he held some kind of cleaning can. In the other he dangled a belt that was neither black nor brown, but aged gray. There was an odor in the air that reminded me of the time I had my tonsils out. Uncle Max, conscious of his dignity as the eldest brother, looked concerned. The office staff, used to these scenes, grinned in anticipation. Whenever a fight started, the standing joke was, "Shall we send for the ambulance or the coroner?"

We pushed through the crowd and I saw Uncle Ed rise from the floor like an apparition.

"Get back," he croaked. "Let me breathe. Let me get at him!"

He snatched the gray belt from Charlie, who overbalanced and fell to the floor. Ed lunged at him. "What are you trying to do? Kill your own brother?"

"Why doesn't anybody listen to me?" Charlie yelled.

"You Cain, you—"

Mannie and Uncle Max held Eddie, while Altman grabbed Uncle Charlie. They were separated with difficulty.

"Quiet down," Mannie ordered. "What happened?"

Uncle Ed, pale and trembling, couldn't stop coughing. Between sputters, he gasped, "Charlie tried to kill me."

"I did no such thing," Charlie protested, his face puckering like a child. "Why doesn't anyone listen to me." He extended a bedraggled belt toward his brother. "All I was trying to do was take off the black dye."

"*Die* is the word," Eddie said, clearing his throat. "The fumes came over to my tasting table like poison gas. I fainted, didn't I? A few more whiffs and I'd be dead."

"Ed, you know I love you." Tears clouded his eyes. "I was going to give you two belts as a surprise."

"A lot of good two belts would do me in a coffin," Eddie sniffed. Then mollified, added, "Okay, forget it."

"That Mr. Hartwick," Uncle Max demanded. "Where is he? Never does what I tell him. Bertha just phoned. She's been waiting hours to be driven to Magnin's. Now she blames me. Says I forgot to tell him."

"Bet he didn't deliver my suitcase," Uncle Eddie said, suddenly mad again.

Mannie calmed his brothers saying that he would deliver Ed's suitcase, drive Bertha to Magnin's, and then take me to Jack's Restaurant for lunch. (The same Jack's, in the same location on Sacramento near Montgomery, is still doing a thriving business today. The decor—plain white tablecloths and brass wall hooks—and even the gray-haired waiters seem unchanged.)

When we finally got to Jack's we were delayed once more at the frosted-glass entrance by a shoe-shine boy who brought over his box and asked, "Mr. Mannie, how about giving you your regular shine?"

Impatiently I watched while the boy snapped his cloth over my father's shoes. "All through," he said at last. Mannie lifted his derby, showing his sparsely covered dome. "Now that you've polished off the bottom, how about the top?" The boy laughed and Mannie tossed him a quarter.

Once inside the restaurant, beclouded by cigar smoke, a gray-haired waiter, with the agility of a youthful fullback, bucked through the knot of customers. As he led the way to a table close to the mirrored wall, my father popped his derby up and down in answer to the greetings of "Hello, Mannie." No sooner were we seated than the waiter presented him with a thin-stemmed glass of sherry and a double-sized menu. Dad handed me the menu.

"Peanuts, this is all in French. You read it." And then, turning to the waiter, he said, "Trois bleu, boom, boom!"

The waiter smiled, *"Oui, oui, monsieur.* The usual, shrimps in the shell, filet of sole meuniere, salad, and cantaloupe."

What I ate, I can no longer remember, but it must have been a huge amount, because when the waiter brought the check I let out a loud burp.

Mannie laughed and said, "Come in."

V

AN EVENING
AT HOME

*L*UNCH OVER, Mannie put me on the Pacific cable car. "Take care of Peanuts," he said, handing me and a nickel to the conductor. The conductor responded with a loud clang of his bell, while Mannie hailed a cab to drive him back to his office.

At the corner of Pacific Avenue and Scott Street, I jumped off the dinkey and ran the short distance to our home. My Mary Jane patents spatted against the pavement, up the stone steps, then clicked against the marble floor of the entrance way.

The changing tap of my shoes reminded me of the game Dad used to play with me when I was little—change tunes. He would run his fingers up and down my back while singing words he'd originated:

> *Up in the mountains, underneath the ground*
> *Where sweet tobacco juice never can be found*
> *Always will remember, so long as don't forget*
> *Put up an umbrella when it is wet.*

When the tickling got to be too much he'd pinch my nose and say, "Change tunes."

Right now, I was filled with the same excitement. I was looking for Taro, our butler, who reminded me of Sessue Hayakawa, the movie actor I'd seen in a film at the nickelodeon. I ran along the parquet floor, and my Mary Janes changed tunes, muted by the Oriental rug in the dining room. I came to a flat stop on the linoleum of the pantry.

It was empty. Spotless, it smelled faintly of wood alcohol, which mother insisted be used to clean her crystal glasses before rinsing them in water. Disappointed, I poked my head into the kitchen where Hulda, a tall bony woman, frowned over six pans covered with wafer-thin dough. Caramel bubbled on the stove.

Doubosh torte! Mannie's family must be coming for dinner. That would please my dad. He was miserable on the evenings mother gathered what he called a cultural mishmash.

It was true. Renée sprinkled people together as though they were salad seasoning. She'd mix a soft-spoken Hindu mystic with a Norwegian sculptor with flaring nostrils, and add a dash of lady whose legs had been tattooed during a visit to the Samoan Islands.

After one such gathering Mannie commented, "I should walk in backward. The guests will think I'm leaving."

But I wasn't interested in dinner. I turned back to the pantry. Taro's key was gone from the shelf. He must be in his room in the basement. For an instant I considered going down to walk along the cement corridor and knock on his door. I'd passed it often enough; even leaned sufficiently close to get a whiff of a strange heady odor. No, I'd better not. Mother had warned me not to invade Taro's privacy. Come to think of it, she'd never cautioned me before about barging in on our succession of maids and cooks.

I sat down on the stepladder and waited. It was only four o'clock, yet outside the fog was gathering over the Pana-

ma Pacific Exposition buildings on the Marina. The Palace of
Fine Arts' pink dome peeped through the fog bank like the
top of Dad's head. Then almost as silently as the fog, Taro
slid into the pantry. I let out a nervous giggle. Taro did not
seem to notice. He walked to the wall and pushed the electric
light button. A beam from the bulb reflected in his burnt
almond eyes. Suddenly I forgot what I wanted to tell Taro
and remembered instead that he never laughed at my father's
jokes. Without knowing why, I wanted to get to my bedroom
with its wallpaper of blue bowknots and pink roses.

I got off the stepladder and started toward the dining
room, but Taro's hand shot out and circled my waist. I stood
there pinned, unable to move. Yet I did move. I was gliding
with Taro in a kind of slow dance rhythm back to the stepladder. He seated himself, then pulled me without effort onto
his lap.

An odd feeling went through me, scary and exciting. I
couldn't take my eyes from Taro's sleek hair. The pungent
odor that came from his room surrounded me; cigarette tobacco and perfumed hair oil mingled with incense. My lips
parted half in astonishment and half with some inner response
that was ready to pop.

"Chérie," Renée called from the dining room. "Hulda
told me you were home."

Before I could answer, Renée came into the pantry. Taro
was even quicker. With the delicacy with which he washed
Renée's fine crystal, he slid me off his lap, and in that same
instant stood courteous, eyes remote, as if he'd been waiting
for her instructions right along.

I couldn't tell if she'd seen anything. "Come upstairs,"
she said to me, "I want to hear all about your day at the
office," and without a change of expression turned to Taro.
"Dinner at seven-thirty. Please use the Limoges."

Limoges was Renée's second best set of china. I was
right. My aunts and uncles were coming to dinner.

They were trooping into the entrance hall. From my bedroom I could hear the laughter and chatter and the greetings of "Good evening, Renée–Hello, Mannie."

Joe, in belted Norfolk jacket and his first pair of long trousers, pushed open my door. "The Brandensteins are coming, tra la tra la. Hurry, Rabbie."

I took a last dissatisfied look at myself in the mirror, at my starched dimity with the lace petticoat that showed beneath the hem, which mother insisted was *très chic* for a *jeune fille* of eleven. How I hated my fluffed out hair with the red bow stuck on top like a cherry on a sundae. I closed my eyes, then opened them at the sound of Uncle Henry's voice booming up the stairwell. He was Dad's attorney brother, whom Dad told me had graduated from Harvard cum laude. I assumed he got the award because of his loud voice.

Anxious as I was to see my aunts and uncles, who were as different from one another as Heinz' fifty-seven varieties, I dreaded to *knix*, the curtsy I was expected to make in front of each, while they in turn inspected me.

I walked slowly down the stairs and hesitated in the doorway of the living room. Seated on the sofa, Renée, in a Fortuni coral hostess gown, her white shoulders bare, looked like a queen presiding over a collection of exuberant pumpkins.

Aunt Tillie noticed me first. "Come over here and get your sensible pills." That was her name for the little peppermints she carried in her evening bag. She was the daintiest and funniest of Dad's sisters. What fascinated me was that she had one glass eye, so perfect one couldn't tell which eye it was. She'd even fooled the doctor during an examination. When he beamed his pencil light into her eye, she said, "Stop wasting your time and my money. You're looking in the wrong one."

On my way over to Aunt Till, Joe, lolling in a chair and grabbing hors d'oeuvres two at a time from the tray our new French maid was passing, knocked my knee. "Don't you look cute, Rabbie. How about bowing to me?"

Dad, who was talking to Uncle Max about coffee sales, turned around. "What did you call your sister?"

Joe blocked an answer by shoving another hors d'oeuvre into his mouth. He need not have bothered. Uncle Eddie interrupted Dad's conversation. "Mannie, you're hipped on coffee promotions. I tell you, put your money on rice. Remember there's a war in Europe and a German blockade of English ships. Till now the English have had a corner on rice deliveries from the Orient. If the war keeps up, rice will be at a premium. We should get on the bandwagon."

"Who knows how long the war will last," Mannie started to argue. He got no further. Mother issued an edict. "Manfred, no business talk here."

Under his breath, Dad muttered, "Pardon me for breathing." For a moment everyone was silent, as though greeting a teacher in class.

Then someone said, "Hear Abe Ruef gets out of San Quentin tomorrow."

At once the chattering started again.

Ever since I could remember, the names Abe Ruef and Mayor Schmitz had drifted in and out of the conversations. I wasn't quite clear about what these two had done, for the grownups left circles of unfinished sentences floating around me. Abe Ruef I knew had been sent to prison for being a bad man, sometime after the earthquake almost ten years ago. He was a boss who had taken a lot of boodle, which I thought meant noodle and wondered what could be so wrong about that. And he was considered twice as bad because he was a Jew. That puzzled me, too. Whenever a man got into trouble and the headlines, the first question the family asked was, "Is he a Jew?"

From the talk I'd overheard, I figured Mayor Schmitz was equally to blame. He'd also taken a lot of boodle. Only he hadn't been sent to jail. Maybe because he wasn't a Jew. He was even trying to be mayor of San Francisco again, though most people agreed he didn't stand a chance against Sunny Jim Rolph.

Now Mannie started to laugh. "Wish Abe Ruef could bring back the good old French restaurants. I had lunch at Pierre's the other day and he was explaining why he'd had to raise the prices on his menu. When Ruef was city boss, things were different; Pierre could afford serving seventy-five-cent family meals downstairs as long as the chandeliers trembled at twenty dollars overhead."

Mother said, "Manfred!"

The others laughed. I couldn't see what was so funny about Mannie's remark. Then I noticed Uncle Henry wasn't smiling either.

"What's the matter, Heinz?" Aunt May said. "Are you still sore about not being elected district attorney back in 1905 when Ruef was the big cheese?"

Uncle Henry's wife, May, dark eyed with the scrubbed complexion of a country girl and the jutting nose of a Roman princess, liked nothing better than to aggravate the husband she adored.

"You always get things wrong, May," Uncle Henry growled. "The only reason I was defeated was because it was the first time we had voting machines in San Francisco. The public didn't know how to operate them. With only two minutes to vote, naturally they pulled the lever with the straight ticket."

"Don't you mean crooked?" Aunt Tillie interrupted.

"I stand corrected," Uncle Henry went on, still not smiling. "Why," he rumbled, "I recall the exact statement I gave out to the newspapers. The *Call*, the *Examiner*, the *Chronicle*, all asked me what I had to say after losing the election." Uncle Henry cleared his throat. "Brandenstein, although defeated, says"—he shook a finger at the company as if they were a jury—"Brandenstein says—"

Uncle Charlie let out a giggle. "Brandenstein says phooey!"

Not to be deflected from the joy of an argument with her husband and the pleasure of shocking the guests, Aunt May persisted. "Voting machines or not, it was Abe Ruef with his smears and his blackmail."

"May!" Aunt Florine pursed her lips and shifted her eyes toward me.

For a moment Aunt May interrupted her usual flow and, opening her evening bag, took out a handkerchief and blew her nose like a trumpet. Blackmail? I had an idea that my Uncle Henry must have received a big black letter from the boss. How could that make him lose the election? It took me a long time to discover what the blackmail was all about. Abe Ruef, knowing Henry to be an ambitious young attorney who planned to show up his graft, had retaliated by circulating a story that Henry Ulysses Brandenstein, true to his middle name, possessed the same craftiness and desire to wander as the mythical Ulysses. This so-called circumspect attorney had married an innocent young woman in order to cover up an affair of long standing with a voluptuous blonde whose reputation was so obvious it could not be questioned. Lie though this was, far from irritating Aunt May it had added pepper to her romance. Nor would she let him forget the incident, making it a point to remind him that he was *un homme fatal.* Oh, Ruef's accusations might not have been proved true, yet could he deny that May's best friend, Maria, had conveniently twisted her ankle right at the entrance of the Brandenstein home as Henry opened the door? Or that Amy, the famed beauty who had once attracted Caruso, insisted that no voice held the throb of Henry's?

Aunt May, having satisfied herself with the blast from her nose, went on to corner her stocky husband like a bull in the ring. "So you're an honest man. You've been everything in this town from honorable supervisor to honorary fire commissioner. As a result you have a nice respectable law practice and a host of stodgy friends. Is that a reward for your virtue?"

This time Dad interrupted with an indignant, "Leave my

brother Henry alone. He has achieved a position in this community none of the rest of us could buy with dollars."

Thrown off the track, Aunt May beat an illogical retreat. "Bah! All of you make me sick with your high principles and conservatism. I'll tell you one thing; I'm bringing up my daughters to be free independent thinkers."

"That's great, May," Uncle Henry rallied for a final shot. "Perhaps it would please you if your daughters grew up to marry IWW's."

Aunt Tillie broke the tension with a pun. "It would be better if they married one of those I. W. Hellmans." (The Hellmans owned the Wells Fargo Bank and they had three sons.)

Uncle Henry, next to Uncle Sol who'd died at seven, was considered the second flower of the family. Whenever I visited their home, where Aunt May always brought out a pot of tea and a plate of cookies into the copper-and-brass-filled living room, I found an excuse to go to the upstairs bathroom.

I'd never seen a bathroom like that before. It was very large and sunny with tied-back, white muslin curtains and window boxes of geraniums. And although the taps did not gleam like ours, and often there were stray hairs in the wash basin, the bathroom was lined all the way round with two-foot-high bookshelves. And that was funny, too, because there were shelves of books in the living room and library that reached all the way to the ceiling, but those in the bathroom were within easy reach even if you were seated. They were foreign books, but I couldn't make out the lettering. Dad told me they were Latin and Greek, and that his brother Henry could speak these languages as fluently as Mother spoke French.

Now Mother caught me staring. "*Fille, fille,* haven't you forgotten to say good evening to someone?"

I looked around the room guiltily. Sure enough, by a rubber plant and partially hidden by a drape stood Uncle A. J. Head bent, he was examining a leaf through both his ribboned pince-nez and a magnifying glass. Uncle A. J. was the smallest of the Brandenstein brothers; so short he'd even shortened his name from Alfred Joseph to the initials A. J. Dad used to say that when A. J. had a pain he didn't know if it came from a corn or a headache. And Dad had told me that as a child A. J. had been caught stealing some peaches from a fruit vendor's cart. The dealer followed the escaping child back to the house and told Pa of the theft. Despite peach juice dribbling down little A. J.'s chin, he denied his guilt. Pa first paid off the vendor, then thundered at the trembling child. "I wouldn't mind if you'd told the truth, but to lie is to cast doubt on the integrity of the Brandensteins." Ever after that day, A. J., with the ghost of Pa hovering over him, was unable to make any statement that wasn't the exact truth. If you asked him the time, he'd take out his watch and say, "It's half past—no—it's twenty-nine and a half minutes past."

Now he bent over a glossy leaf of the rubber plant and muttered, "I think there are bugs on this one. I'm not sure."

"Oh, Uncle A. J.," I apologized, "I didn't see you."

Immediately, I knew I'd offended him. He stretched as though he, not the plant, were rubber. He cleared his throat. But whatever he was about to say was interrupted by Taro's appearance in the doorway to announce dinner. He didn't glance my way but stood, head bowed, waiting for the company. Now I must say good night, and I'd hardly finished saying good evening.

I kissed Mother, then went over to Mannie, who was whispering to Uncle Max. "Listen, I've got an idea for a great coffee promotion." Dad turned to hug me absently. The only time my father didn't pay attention to me was when he talked about coffee.

Mother rose from the sofa. "Dinner, Manfred," she said and led my aunts and uncles into the dining room. I waited till Taro followed and closed the French doors, whose glass was covered halfway up with café au lait-colored, embroidered curtains.

I started up the staircase, then paused at the curve to

look down. To my amazement I saw Uncle A. J. still standing outside the shut dining-room doors. His head did not quite clear the curtained division. Tentatively he reached for the knob, then withdrew his hand into his pocket. He stood on tiptoes; his shoes squeaked and his pince-nez fell from his tiny nose to dangle forlornly on the black ribbon. How I wished I could bring him Taro's stepladder so he could climb it and be seen through the glass partition.

It was Mannie who came to the rescue. He opened the door. "A. J., why didn't you come along with the others?"

I could hear Mother's voice, imperious, "Manfred, don't jump up from the table. Taro's the one to attend to our guests."

Taro packed his suitcase the following day. I tried to tell myself he'd been dismissed because he'd forgotten A. J. behind the dining-room curtains. I didn't want to remember Taro's taking me on his lap. Mother said no more to me about Taro. She was gentle with me and hugged me a lot that afternoon and called me her *bébé*.

When Dad came home, he didn't mention Taro either. And he didn't kiss me. His eyes seemed to measure me for a moment before he touched my cheek lightly and, calling me Ruth instead of Peanuts, said, "It takes two to dance the gadzodsky."

Dad had used a funny word, but I knew he didn't expect me to laugh.

VI

FOURTH OF JULY

What, what happened on the Fourth of July?
Johnson gave Jeffries a punch in the eye.

IF ADVERTISING promotion was a new story to me, it was an old one to Mannie. Before the days of the flannel-suit boys, he was the adman in a derby hat. He believed in ballyhoo. Ballyhoo was the first cousin of the theater, which he loved. And in 1910 came his big chance.

At the last minute, the Jeffries-Johnson prizefight was shifted from San Francisco to Reno. Mannie knew he could get away with a lot in Reno that he would never dare try in San Francisco.

One morning at the office, Mannie told his brother Max, "I've got two ringside seats for the fight. I want to take one of our coffee salesmen with me."

"A salesman," Max echoed, "at forty-five dollars a ducat? What's wrong with your own brother?"

"No, no Max. It'll be hotter than the hinges and you know you can't stand the heat. I'd like someone from the coffee department. Maybe Sandy Swann."

"Are you mad, Mannie? He's just an eighteen-year-old kid. Only been moved from the packing plant for a tryout in sales a couple of months ago."

"I've been watching him," Mannie said, as if gazing into a crystal ball. "He's a salesman with latent talent."

Max's protests made his round cheeks quiver. It would, he pointed out, make Altman, the senior sales manager, too sore to live with if Mannie took Sandy to Reno. Max went back to his office muttering. At the door he turned around. "All you think about is coffee. What about rice, what about tea? Let me tell you, Mannie, if you have some crazy promotion up your sleeve, remember I'm not my brother's keeper."

Sandy's hair, like his name, was the off-color red of an Airedale's. He had a way of keeping his flecked eyes on you— even me—no matter what you said, and he made me feel smart. He favored an orange necktie. I remember his necktie because one day when he was invited to our home he asked Renée if she thought it was too loud.

"I don't know," my mother answered, "I'm hard of hearing."

It was the first time Renée had ever made a joke, and none of us ever forgot her punch line.

Mannie had gathered around him over a period of time a crew of what he called supersalesmen. Some drank too much, and had to be protected from the sober, punctilious Mr. Altman. To Dad, what counted was, could they sell? He had his own system of judging a man's ability. Could he play baseball? If so, he would know when to hold onto the ball and when to throw it, when to press a sale and when to hold back.

On the day Sandy Swann first walked into Mannie's office he stood there awkwardly, his big hands working over a checked cap. With eyes intent as a boy's, he explained he'd been a jitney driver and used to pass the big MJB COFFEE WHY? sign on his run from Market Street to the Southern Pacific Depot. He just wondered if he could perhaps—Dad lit a cigarette and startled Sandy by asking if he'd ever played baseball. Sandy's eyes widened and he quit torturing his cap. Yes. He'd belonged to the Market sandlot team. Won four out of five games against the Mission Tigers. The last game he'd pitched was a tough one. He stopped short, the flecked eyes on my father. No need to apologize, Mannie told him, baseball happened to be one of his favorite sports. Would he like to start with a job in the MJB packing plant? The answering grin on Sandy's face showed the spaces between his white teeth. Mannie smiled to himself. Sandy was his man all right.

Sandy's eyes lit up when Mannie showed him the fight tickets and asked if he would drive him to Reno. Mannie enjoyed being mysterious; he gave no explanation. Sandy knew when to hold onto the ball and he did not ask questions. The fight was to take place on Monday. Sandy, in the company car, parked in front of our home at six-thirty Saturday morning. Mannie came down the steps swinging one arm and looking over his shoulder at the sky. No fog. If the weather held out, it would be a scorcher in Reno on the Fourth.

Sandy hadn't been a jitney driver for nothing. Apart from the engine boiling at Donner Pass, they made a fast trip and reached Reno by three o'clock. The outlying roads were filled with ruts and hogbacks. Reno was still a mining town. But that day it lived up to its future boast—The Biggest Little City in the World. The streets were bursting with what Mannie described as a motley crew. Men and women pushing, panting, and waiting to see the fight that would prove once and for all no Negro could capture a title from a white man.

Virginia Street was going full blast to the click of pool balls and the rattle of dice. Cowboys in high-heeled boots and silver-studded belts swaggered past painted ladies in high-heeled button shoes and hobble skirts. City reporters elbowed each other. Big-bosomed and big-hipped women had deserted their night haunts to blink in the unaccustomed light of day. Mannie urged Sandy to get through the crowds and on to the hotel. There was work to be done.

Once he and Sandy were settled at the Golden Hotel, Mannie took off his collar and ordered a couple of beers. He opened the windows. Below, the birch trees were motionless. The Truckee River had shrunk to a trickle over the rocks. Mannie, who hated heat, relished it now. The stage was set. It was time to let go with the plot.

Sandy sat on the davenport sipping from his schooner.

"Sandy," my father said, "you're my boy. You made Reno in plenty of time."

Sandy nodded and took another slow sip.

"But that's only part of the point."

Sandy felt this was the moment to ask, "What's the whole point?"

"When we've both cooled off a bit, I'll go visit the groceries. Hear some of the other brands are giving us stiff competition. That's not bothering me. I like a good opponent, especially when I've got an ace in the hole. Greatest captive audience in the world right here for the next few days."

Sandy kept his eyes on Mannie and waited.

"What I want you to do is go to a paint shop. Buy all the cans of green paint and white paint you can lay your hands on. After you've done that, go round up all the fans you can find."

Sandy's eyebrows shot up, and Mannie laughed. "Not fight fans. The raffia ones to blow away the heat."

If Sandy was puzzled he gave no further sign.

My father warmed to the scheme. "You've got to work fast, boy. I heard you can handle paints and a brush, as well as sell coffee. You'd better buy some brushes. Here," he reached into his pocket, "this fifty should cover your expenses. If you run short have them charged to Mannie Brandenstein at the Golden Hotel. I'll leave word to okay it with the desk clerk. Now here are your work orders. Once you've got the fans and the paint, come back to the room and start lettering the fans with big MJB COFFEE WHY? signs."

Sandy set down his beer mug. "Shall I get going?"

"Fast but not so fast. That's only half of the story. I figure it will take most of tonight and part of tomorrow to paint the fans. Sunday's the big day. Maybe I should say Saturday night. By that time everybody'll be busy placing last minute bets and celebrating in advance. Even the police, such as they are, will keep one eye shut.

"Now, get this. The open air arena is a few blocks out of town. At ten o'clock at night, the streets on that side of town should be empty and the saloons and gambling joints downtown full. I want you to paint the sidewalks from the railroad station to the fight ring with green footprints. Between the steps put big white question marks and the MJB letters."

Mannie took out a tube of menthol and inhaled it while he watched Sandy. He was rewarded with a big grin. Sandy jammed the checked cap over his Airedale hair and went for the door.

"Whoa! Two more pieces of instruction. Tonight when you get back to your room, order yourself a Delmonico steak dinner. And here's a five spot for you. Stop off at Corbett's poolroom and place a bet that Jeffries will be knocked out before the eighteenth round. It's a long shot, but I got a hunch you could make some money."

Well, everything went off like a movie reel unwinding, except that Sunday morning Dad nearly suffocated from the stink of raffia, varnish, and paint. Fans, fans, fans were spread all over the room and tacked to the walls. Sandy sprawled limp as a puppet on the davenport, a yellow betting ticket tucked under his head.

When he finally woke up, he told Mannie he'd had no trouble painting the sidewalks. No sheriffs around. And the few stragglers were only mildly curious. One thing bothered Sandy. A green blob of paint stained his jacket.

"Forget it," Mannie kidded. "You painted the town red and yourself green!"

Early on the morning of the fight, Mannie and Sandy came down the elevator carrying a couple of cartons filled with fans.

In the hotel bar four sportswriters were arguing the odds over neat shots of whiskey. "Eight to five on Jeffries. He's the 'white hope.'"

"Naw," another protested, "Jeffries' been fishing, not training. Big boy Johnson's got a powerful right."

Dad and Sandy hustled past with their cartons. No one turned a head. Voices grew louder, with a constant refrain bandied about—the "white hope."

More out of wishful thinking than reason, the odds were on Jeffries. That a white man should fight a Negro was unusual in the early 1900s. Jeffries had been brought out of retirement to put an end to the Negro's alarming streak of victories. Trains and boxcars loaded with people from all over the United States kept arriving at the Reno station. The public whetted its collective appetite in anticipation of seeing Johnson go down in a slugging match they hoped would go fifty rounds.

Mannie and Sandy pushed their way past the crowds at the station to walk the three blocks to the arena. The green footsteps on the pavement shone like fluorescent paint under the already hot sun. The question marks shimmered between the letters MJB.

Only one job left to do. Find some kids who would give out fans at the entrance gate. For a dime à la Rockefeller, big fists and small and grubby ones fought one another in an unscheduled fight to distribute the fans.

In their ringside seats, Mannie and Sandy sat down to watch the fight of the century.

It turned out to be a disappointment from the moment Jeffries took off his robe to reveal a fat and flabby body. In the second round, Johnson, gold teeth shining and his brown body glistening, landed a punch that started to close Jeffries' eye. Jeffries wilted rather than sagged against the ropes.

But if the fight was a flop, Mannie's campaign was a great success. The more the audience booed and sweltered, the more they waved their fans, till the air became a fanning wall of MJB COFFEE WHY?s.

The fight lasted fifteen instead of fifty rounds, and Johnson's final right to the jaw was the end of the "white hope."

Sandy clutched his bet ticket and rushed away to collect. Just like a kid, Mannie thought, watching the check cap bob up and down between the spectators. No wonder the boy was excited. On the five dollars my father had given him to place the bet, he stood to cash in one hundred and ten dollars.

"Meet you at the Golden!" Mannie yelled after him.

Sandy turned his head for an instant and collided with an enormous cerise taffeta bow shooting off a straw hat. In the distance Mannie saw Sandy take off his cap and bow his Airedale head in apology. Then he was lapped up by the cerise bow.

The heat subsided, but not the shouting. Amateur referees argued the blows, a band pranced in the streets, the crowd left the arena holding onto their MJB fans for souvenirs. Back in his hotel room Mannie ordered two *filets mignons, béarnaise* sauce and a bottle of sparkling Burgundy; Sandy had not let him down. They could relax. Tomorrow they would visit the grocery stores.

The waiter brought the dinner, set the table, and with a deferential bow he accepted the bright Nevada silver dollar Mannie tossed him.

Outside, the St. Mary's church bells chimed seven o'clock.

Where was Sandy? Why hadn't he shown up? Could he be roaming the bars, throwing away his winnings on the green tables? Or could he have been trapped by the cerise bow? After all he was only eighteen.

Mannie left the food untouched. He grabbed his derby. He'd find the boy if it took all night. Up and down Virginia Street he went, in and out of the Bonanza, the Bucket of Blood, and the Saddle and Spur. He covered all of them. Nowhere could he find the Airedale head, nor had anyone been seen matching the description. He left the bright orange lights to find the dimmer red ones on the outskirts of town. But in each ornate parlor with its fancy chandelier and the piano against the beaded curtains, the answer was no!

Mannie went back to the hotel and called Reno General Hospital. He drew a blank. There could be only one possibility left—the town jail. Dad ran all the way to the little adobe jail across from the courthouse.

A fat desk sergeant swatted flies and chewed on a dead cigar.

"I don't want to interrupt your safari," Mannie apologized breathlessly. "By any chance, did a fellow with reddish hair and freckles happen this way? His name is Sandy Swann."

Sandy was behind bars. He had collected his money, and beguiled by the cerise taffeta bow, had fallen on evil times at the Gold Nugget. Cleaned out by several shots at the bar, champagne for the lady and a few bets, he had gotten into an argument with, of all people, a man wearing a silver star. The green paint on Sandy's jacket matched the green on the Reno sidewalks and the coffee salesman was under arrest. He had refused to phone Mannie and involve the MJB Company.

Mannie surveyed him as he lay groaning on the broken springs of the jail mattress. Mannie put up bail and half-carried Sandy back to the hotel.

The next morning at nine o'clock, Mannie and a chastened Sandy stood before what the desk sergeant had warned them was a pro tem judge, fresh out of law school. His Honor studied the dossier and began what Mannie termed a *langweilige Spiel* on all the crimes committed by the visitor from San Francisco.

Mannie interrupted him politely.

"If anyone's to blame, Your Honor, I am."

"And who are you?"

"I'm Mannie—Mr. Manfred Brandenstein, a partner of the MJB Coffee Company."

The judge held up a pudgy hand.

"Perhaps you think names impress me, Mr. Branden-stein," he said curtly. "You're a businessman of importance in San Francisco. No doubt you know Judge Max Sloss, newly appointed to the California Supreme Court. He might put in a good word for you."

Mannie smiled blandly. "The judge speaks very highly of you, Your Honor."

The judge dropped his languid hand.

"Speaks highly of me?" he echoed. "Well, I must admit I admire him, too." He adjusted the collar of his black robe and squared his shoulders. "I really don't think the judge remembers me," he went on. "I was present at a bar association dinner in San Francisco—happened to pass the judge the salt for his celery. I wonder if he does remember me." His eyes dropped to the dossier again.

"I'm sure he does, Your Honor," Mannie murmured.

"Where did you say the deputy made his charge?" the Judge asked Sandy.

"At the Gold Nugget, Your Honor."

"Tut-tut! At the Gold Nugget, you say? Was the deputy by any chance indulging in a libation?"

"He was, Your Honor."

"I will see that he is properly admonished," His Honor observed, aware that he had stumbled on a dignified exit. "As for you, young man, fifty dollars should cover the cost of having the paint removed from the sidewalks."

Mannie hastily forked over the greenbacks before the Judge could change his mind. He cleared his throat and, always the actor, bowed deferentially toward the youthful pro tem judge.

"Your Honor, permit me to send you a case of MJB coffee."

Pro tem lifted his hand and spread his pudgy fingers.

"No bribery here, sir," he said.

"Of course not, Your Honor. Just wanted you to enjoy

the same coffee Judge Sloss drinks."

Pro tem so far forgot himself as to scratch his head.

"Do you really think His Honor remembers me?" he murmured. He went on, with a benign smile turned inward on itself, "Speaks very highly— could be at that."

Mannie and Sandy hurried out of the courtroom.

By 1917, as had been predicted after the earthquake, San Francisco had risen like a phoenix out of the ashes. The business section was solidly rebuilt with fireproof buildings, firm and tall, but not yet reaching today's high rises. The MJB Company had moved to concrete quarters that took up half of Third Street catercorner to the mission-style Southern Pacific Depot (since torn down), where the commuter trains, the Lark and the Sunset Limited, blasted their whistles.

The lower floor of the MJB building was given over to offices, with an open section for tea and coffee testing. Mr. Hartwick had been promoted to his own desk in the center, from which snaked cords connected to three telephones. The bells rang continuously, and like a juggler, Mr. Hartwick picked up one receiver then another, answering orders from the brothers, their wives, and now their children. On the second floor, around which ran a gallery, Sandy had an office whose frosted-glass door was lettered, Senior Sales Manager. He had replaced Mr. Altman, who one day collapsed behind his desk like a vacuum-packed tin punctured with air. Sandy's manner was no longer awkward. But if he hid the freckled-faced boy he'd been, he hadn't buried him. His flecked eyes still had a trick of making you think you were talking to a kid instead of a supersalesman. His Airedale hair was smooth now.

My father's promotions had smoothed down, too—less spectacular, but he hadn't given them up. In the west wing of the second floor was a cafeteria and lounge. A lady decorator had been engaged to create the proper atmosphere for the

Central American coffee and Oriental tea served there. When Mannie first beheld her flight of fancy, which was a blast of orange and yellow tables, pagoda-shaped chairs, and mystic black scrolls on the drapes, he slapped his forehead, declaring, "Looks like a joss house!"

Every Friday afternoon Mannie put on a *Kaffeeklatsch* with a vaudeville show directed by him using the employees as actors. Sandy, the salesman, was what Mannie called a natural-born, soft-shoe dancer, his loose body as relaxed as a marionette on a string. I remember that once when I was allowed to watch a show, I forgot to eat my doughnut because Sandy seemed to be dancing just for me. Everybody was having a great time, until one day Uncle Max protested. "Mannie, no one's working around here anymore. The factory workers, the sales force, the stenographers, are always in rehearsal. Even Mr. Hartwick refused to drive me to the Argonaut Club for lunch yesterday. He said he had to get you some costumes. This has got to stop! We are not running a theater. We're in business."

My father and Uncle Max were off to their yelling routine. Uncle Ed and Uncle Charlie popped out of their offices. Uncle A. J. opened his door and shut it again like a jack-in-the-box. The typists came to a dead halt on the keys, waiting. Mr. Mannie must win. With his coaching, each felt it was only a matter of time before they would be discovered by Belasco.

Mannie shook his head. He wasn't going to give up show biz. "Hold your horses, Max. I'll come up with an idea."

"I'm sick of your ideas. There'll be no more *Kaffeeklatsches* or acting and that's final!"

That might have been the end of it had it not been for Sandy. Why not, he suggested smoothly, open the *Kaffeeklatsch* to the public? The grocers could give away tickets to their customers who bought MJB products. So, without a blink from his flecked eyes, he pacified Max and satisfied Mannie. Sales went up and the shows went on.

VII

PSYCHIATRIST
WITHOUT COUCH

*O*NE SUNDAY afternoon when Mother and Joe had gone to the Palace of Fine Arts at the Exposition to view an exhibition of French impressionists, I opened the library door and found Dad alone in a leather chair smoking a cigarette. I settled myself on a footstool at his feet. Now was my chance to learn about sales and advertising in his coffee world. To my eager questions, Mannie laughed. "Whoa, Sarsaparilla! All that can be answered with one word, 'psychology.' That's a highfalutin word," he went on, "so let me tell you how it works."

He put out his cigarette, paused for effect, then began a story about one of his crackerjack salesmen, who, try as he would, was unable to sell our brand of coffee to a leading grocery outfit. He'd talked to the top man but had made no headway. He was so tough, the salesman told Mannie, he wouldn't accept the coffee if we gave it away.

"He was right, Peanuts," Mannie said. "I called on the top man myself. He was as hard as the Rock of Gibraltar."

"What did you do?"

Mannie needed no prompting. "If a man won't let you do him a favor, there's only one way to get around the mulberry bush. You've got to let him do *you* a favor. I happened to know that this tough character admired baseball players, so I started talking about Ty Cobb and Christy Mathewson. Then I casually mentioned I was going to New York on business during the World Series, and how impossible it was to get tickets. Suddenly he melted like a snowbank in a July heat wave. 'Mannie,' he said, 'let me present you with two box seats.' And," Dad concluded, "before I left his office, he placed an order for a carload of coffee." Mannie's moustache curved upwards to show his white teeth. "That's how I cracked the Rock of Gibraltar."

Dad must have noticed my rapt expression for he said, "I don't want you to think your father is 'in-faaliaable.' " He went on to tell me how once he'd outsmarted himself. He'd offered a grocer a new suit if the grocer could empty his shelves of our coffee in a week. The grocer accepted the challenge and cleared the shelves within a week. Now Dad started to laugh. "How could I know he was going to order a $250 suit from the best tailor in town?"

Evidently the experience had taught Mannie a lesson. When next he made an offer to another grocer, he told him he would buy him a set of furniture if he, too, could sell the coffee within a certain time. Sure enough the grocer did. Dad sent him a set of furniture—all miniatures.

I was laughing, too. Then serious once more, I said, "Tell me about advertising."

Dad reached for another cigarette with a dramatic gesture. As young as I was, I realized he was an actor—the kind who thought of himself as the whole show, like the man I'd seen at the Orpheum who changed hats behind a screen to play different parts.

Mannie laid his cigarette on the indentation of the copper ashtray. "Almost forgot you were here, Peanuts. All selling is a kind of advertising. You've got to understand the buyer. Now, if a man comes into my office to buy coffee beans, the first thing I do is size him up. If he's already made up his mind to buy the best quality and is willing to pay the price, then there's no problem. But if he looks like he has the money for the best and wants to get away with buying the cheapest, that's when I have to use psychology."

"How?"

"Well, I bring in three grades of coffee beans on three different trays. The most expensive grade I put on the simplest tray, the middle price on a little fancier tray, and the cheapest on a brightly decorated one. I put the cheapest on my desk practically under his nose. The middle price I put a little farther away on a table, and the most expensive I put on a shelf in the corner. Then I point to the fancy tray on my desk and tell him here are beans that will suit his price. Right away his eyes wander to the tray on the table. 'How about those beans?' 'Better grade,' I answer, 'probably more than you want to pay.' 'And those?' he says, looking at the simple tray on the shelf. 'Oh, those are top quality beans, way beyond your price.' Then I make him smell the beans on my desk and keep repeating these are the beans he wants. The more I talk, the more his eyes wander. First he studies the pile of green beans on the table, then he seems unable to take his eyes off the beans on the simple tray that I put way up on the shelf. Invariably he ends up insisting on buying the high-price beans that I've made no effort to sell. So," Mannie chuckled, "I close a deal I'd been wanting to make from the start."

"You haven't told me about slogans," I said, proud of the new word I'd heard over and over during *It Pays to Advertise*, the first real play I'd ever seen.

Mannie took out a tube of New Skin from his pocket and carefully covered a minute scratch with it. It was a kind of medical Scotch tape. Another of his favorite remedies was a menthol and eucalyptus oil he pressed to his nostrils from a tube. These odors I always associate with him, and they seem to last longer than the sound of his laughter. He was no hypochondriac, but medication without doctors was for him like finding gold without prospecting.

"There are good slogans and bad ones," he went on. "Let's see, Peanuts, if you can judge. Ready?"

I nodded eagerly.

"Well, one of the salesmen came into my office the other day. He had an idea for a coffee billboard. He showed me the layout. It was a drawing of a little colored boy lying in a four-poster bed. The small black head peeped out from under a big, white counterpane. The slogan was A Small Black, and under this was a picture of a demitasse and the letters MJB."

"Oh," I said, delighted I understood the joke, "what a wonderful idea."

Mannie rubbed his finger to see if the New Skin had dried. "Not wonderful at all."

"Why not?"

"First of all, we want to sell our coffee to as many people as possible, and you won't do it that way. But there's a more important reason. You and I belong to a minority and we should be the last to poke fun at another minority. Jewish people don't laugh at pictures of themselves counting money any more than the Scotch enjoy being called cheap or the Irish like cartoons that show them bashing each other over the head. Jokes like these are a mean disguise for prejudice."

I frowned.

"Maybe you're too young to understand the word, or maybe you've not come up against it yet, but what prejudice means is something like all the dark-haired people thinking they're better than the redheads, and trying to push them around. We're fortunate because we happen to live in San Francisco where there's hardly any Jewish prejudice. Your Uncle Max is a director of the Panama Pacific Exposition, there's talk of appointing your Uncle Ed to the National Tea Board, and as you know," Mannie went on with special pride, "my brother Henry is a friend of all the top judges. In other places it isn't the same. Poor Jewish immigrants live in crowded tenements, and the rich Jews are not allowed to visit some of the swank hotels. Even here things may change, so you'll have to be patient and not let yourself be hurt or go around with a chip on your shoulder. Be proud of what you are, but don't ram it down other people's throats." Suddenly Mannie laughed. "I sound like Polonius giving advice to his son, only you happen to be my favorite daughter." For an instant he studied my face. "You're growing up, Peanuts, and you won't be protected all your life. So far you've had it easy and most people would say, 'The world is your oyster.' That isn't how I'd put it. It's more like a steamed clam bordelaise full of sharp flavor. It will be up to you to find the right fork to open it up."

I only half-grasped the meaning of my father's words, and the changes he predicted were so slow in coming I hardly noticed them at the time. Not till my second year in high school did I hear remarks like, "For a Jewish girl you're pretty good looking," and "I like you even if you are Jewish." Remembering what Dad had told me about picking the right fork, I picked other friends. Now I shifted uncomfortably on my footstool.

"What's the matter, Peanuts? Do you want me to change tunes?"

Then, without waiting for my answer, he went on to tell me about Mr. Gillick, a man who made Gillick tops to fit over touring cars. These could be pulled up in the rain, and Mr. Gillick guaranteed they were as solid as a roof on a house. He'd stand behind his product, he told my father, urging him to buy both the touring car and the top. If what Mr. Gillick said was true, Mannie told him he had a customer. First he wanted to test the top. Mannie excused himself and went to find Mr. Hartwick. Mr. Hartwick had been a prizefighter before taking the job of chauffeur *en masse* to all the MJB brothers. If anyone could test the Gillick top he could.

Mannie brought him out to the street where Mr. Gillick had parked the red touring car with the unbreakable roof.

"Give it your knock-out punch," Mannie told Mr. Hartwick.

Mr. Hartwick took a roundhouse swing at the shiny cover and it caved in like a tent in a typhoon.

"You see, Peanuts," Mannie said, laughing. "Never guarantee a product if you can't stand or sit behind it. You've got to deliver quality."

"Our coffee does," I said in a my-father-is-the-best voice.

"So do a lot of other good coffees. That's why you have to outthink them." Dad leaned toward me and whispered, "Between you, me, and the lamp post, MJB is coming out with a new vacuum-packed tin. Now are you sausage-fied?"

"How wonderful. All your problems are over."

"Peanuts, in business nobody's problems are over. You just climb up one hill and then another. Right now we're at the top."

The sunlight had begun to grow dim. Dad got up and pulled the beaded chain on the Tiffany lamp. It was then that Mother walked into the sitting room. She was alone. Joe had already given up culture to run down the hall and phone his latest girl friend. .

I looked at Mother. She was glowing, like the Tower of Jewels, whose multicolored glass panels streamed ribbons of light over the Exposition. She was wearing an accordian-pleated, blue crepe de Chine dress with a foulard scarf tied high on her neck. She seemed more beautiful every time I saw her.

Dad's warm smile of admiration reminded me of the small bronze statue at the fair, *The Little Duck Baby*, who cuddled a duck in his arms with the pride of love and possession.

"Manfred," Renée said, "I've seen the most marvelous paintings today. Nothing like the Keith and Rollo Peters in our living room. Full of life and color—Monet, Manet, Pissarro—but I know you could not possibly be interested."

"Hold your horses!" Mannie said. He took out his little black notebook. "Your French is remarkable, but spell out the trois bleu boom boom names for me."

Renée's birthday was in August. Presents were distributed after supper. I was allowed champagne and a double helping of angel food cake. Mannie gave her a Magnin's box. Inside was a mesh bag made of tiny jade beads, with a gold tassel that jingled.

Renée said, "Manfred, it's lovely. Only I have three evening bags already. I hope you don't mind—"

I winced. But Mannie didn't seem surprised. He looked at Renée as if she had been given the cue line.

"Of course I don't mind," Mannie said calmly. "Return it as usual. But suppose we all go into the drawing room for a while."

Mannie led the way. The room was dark. Renée didn't believe in wasting electricity. My father went over to the wall and pressed the button. The lights came on and I heard Mother gasp. She was looking at the far end of the room.

Against the cream-colored walls, in dull, gold-carved frames, were three paintings, paintings such as I had never seen before; they were real and yet not real. One was a snow scene done in low-key; one a coast, which might have been Monterey, with pale blue ocean and chrome mountains and just a suggestion of foam. The last one was a mass of colors—

blue, greens, and yellows, as though the painter had splashed them on without thought of how they landed. In the center was a fountain spewing water from an old well.

"Renée," Mannie said, "I hope you like your birthday present. The evening bag was only an "hors doovray." I sent a check to your cousin Marcelle in Paris and asked her to select three paintings from the list you gave me." He pulled the black notebook from his pocket. "Monet, Manet, and Pissarro."

For a minute I thought that Mother, controlled as she always was, might giggle or burst into tears.

She did neither. Instead she kissed me and said, "Do you realize what a wonderful father you have?"

"Renée, don't scold me for spending money," Mannie said. Unable to resist pride in a good deal and though he seldom mentioned cost, he went on. "I sent five thousand to Marcelle. She picked these and sent me back four hundred and thirty-five dollars."

Renée's eyes kept sweeping from one to another of the framed pictures. "Oh, Manfred," she said, "I'll never forget this birthday!"

For once she didn't seem to think that her husband had pitched money out the window. And as I saw my father's pleasure, I wondered if he realized that Mother, in all innocence, had used his one-word secret of salesmanship—psychology. On the afternoon when she'd walked into the library to tell him about the French impressionists and had insisted he couldn't possibly be interested, she'd sold him a bill of goods.

VIII

THE SLEUTH

MANNIE FANCIED himself a detective. His only missing props were a peaked cap and a magnifying glass.

On one occasion, when we were comfortably settled at the Blackstone in Chicago, he took Joe and me to a full-course dinner. On our return, he reached for his Patek Phillippe platinum pocket watch, as thin as a worn dime, from his vest pocket. It was missing. He went through our room at the Blackstone like the approved storybook detective, turning out drawers, lifting up rugs, probing the upholstered sofa and chairs. Suddenly he snapped his fingers. He recalled he had been jostled at the restaurant. Renée suggested he call the police.

"The police?" Mannie snorted. "I can do a better job than they can any day!"

He left our hotel early next morning with a predatory look in his eyes. He was going to hunt down the criminal himself. He was gone all day and half the night and he returned empty-handed. It took a long time to drag the story from him. He had purchased a fair imitation of his Patek Phillippe watch for five dollars and a genuine platinum chain for fifty dollars. That, he thought, would really fool the thief. A genuine watch chain was sure to be attached to the real McCoy.

He had gone back to the restaurant and flaunted the watch, convinced that easy pickings would encourage the thief to return. He had even said to himself aloud, shaking the watch, "Hang it all, those fancy jobs from Paris never work!"

But there were no takers. He suddenly remembered while eating lunch that he had taken in a movie before our dinner date, and he got to the Majestic Theatre as quickly as possible. Here in the waiting lines he attracted plenty of attention and marked down some likely characters, one a man with a classic limp and the other an older man with a livid bruise over one eye. He spent a very busy afternoon trying to sit next to both of them in different parts of the house. The outcome was that he lost the genuine chain and returned to Renée with the five-dollar watch.

"Guess today was not my lucky one," he confessed, his face downcast.

Three weeks after our return to San Francisco, he received his watch from the Chicago Police. Renée, despite Mannie's warning not to do so, had informed them of the loss. Fingering the watch, he insisted, "If we had stayed in Chicago another few days I would have found it without any police interference."

Secretly, I hoped he'd have better luck next time. I thought the opportunity would occur when Uncle Charlie, a few days later, called our home, and I picked up the receiver.

"There's been a three-thousand-dollar robbery at MJB!" he yelled. "Get Mannie on the line. He'll catch the thief!"

When I learned a little later that Mr. Hartwick, the button-nose messenger, was missing from the MJB office, I jumped with fright. It was unthinkable that any of the office

staff should lack "integrity." Even the very lowest rungs of
the business ladder at MJB were occupied by people in whom
inordinate trust was reposed. For instance, in the old days
Felix the office boy, who was paid a small salary, was given a
horse and buggy once a month to go to the Nevada Bank,
then on the corner of Sansome and Bush streets, to draw fifteen thousand dollars in gold. He proceeded from the bank to
the customs office where he paid this sum as duty on company imports from China and Japan.

All the same, I reflected, the case of the missing Mr.
Hartwick was worthy of Mannie's best sleuthing talents. He
saw himself as a mixture of Sherlock Holmes and Bulldog
Drummond, with emphasis on the Bulldog.

First Mannie and his brother Charlie went into a huddle
at the office, where all Charlie could do was groan about his
own responsibility in the affair.

"You mean, Charlie, you're the thief," Mannie said, setting his bowler at the right detective rake. "All right, turn
yourself in. I'll stand by my kid brother!"

"Nobody listens to me!" Charlie yelled. "Three thousand dollars disappeared between Friday noon and Friday at
five o'clock. Mannie, you'll simply have to catch the thief
before Monday. I won't have Max and Eddie on my neck. I
refuse to be the scapegoat!"

"Why, Charlie," Mannie asked, his mind concentrating
on who was in the office on Friday afternoon, "why don't
you phone Miss Alanson?"

"Don't you know Sweetie-Pie's on vacation?"

"Hmm!" Mannie was twirling his moustache. The ef-
ficient bookkeeper was on vacation. The plot was thickening.
This was going to be a tough case. "Quit worrying, Charlie,"
he went on. "I'll have the money back by Monday morning,
even if I have to put the three thousand greenbacks in the
safe myself!"

Uncle Charlie's face lit up as if Mannie had been transformed into a shaggy St. Bernard carrying a keg of brandy around his neck.

"I know you can do it, Mannie," Charlie said emotionally. "Nobody listens to me. But people listen to you—and they tell you things!"

It was a very thoughtful Mannie who returned home that evening. I heard my parents talking and Renée said, "Money no object as usual, Manfred. Now you're going to replace that money out of your own pocket."

"Have no fear, Renée," my father replied. "I'll find that money." His voice lacked its usual upbeat tones.

I was horrified. Mannie seemed to have lost his confidence. He went on to say, "Can't understand it. Mr. Hartwick's phone doesn't answer. There's no record of a three thousand dollar withdrawal. I went all over the plant, both upstairs and down. No broken locks, no broken windows, no signs of a struggle."

"Then it must be what you call an inside job," Renée said firmly.

I thought it was time to enter the library where they were talking.

"What are you going to do?" I asked my father.

"I'll bet my bottom dollar that no employee of ours would take that money!" Mannie asserted. "Yet, where is Mr. Hartwick?"

"Yes, where is he?" Renée echoed.

"I've got to do some more thinking," my father said. He took out a wrapped paper containing Seidlitz powder, unfolded it and shook it onto his tongue.

"Renée, if you'll forgive me I'm going to bed."

"With the mystery unsolved?" I asked, aware that Mannie was very tired.

"Peanuts," he said, "I've done all I can tonight. Mr. Hartwick is supposed to pick me up in the morning at eight-thirty to take me to the office. Maybe he knows something I don't."

"If he shows up!" Renée said, and I could tell by the tight line of her lips that her mind was more on Mannie's promise to Uncle Charlie to replace the money than on Mr. Hartwick.

I was up early Monday morning. Mannie was already at the breakfast table. I loved to watch him eat his boiled eggs. He made a ceremony of breaking toast into the egg, which had to be boiled exactly three and one-half minutes, salting and peppering the blend, and then sipping it on his spoon. This morning I was more interested in watching my father's face. He did not seem worried.

"Peanuts," he announced, "I have a feeling I'm on the verge of a solution."

At promptly eight-thirty the doorbell rang. Dad jumped up from the table and, still holding his napkin, beat our new maid to the door.

Mr. Hartwick stood there grinning. "Mannie," he said, "congratulate me, I'm in business!"

"You're not quitting MJB?"

"Who said anything about quittin'? I'm supplementin'. Working weekends only and thanks to you."

"Thanks to me?"

"Remember about six months ago I told you I'd like to go into the secondhand automobile business? You said, 'Mr. Hartwick, any time you need some cash to get started just go to Miss Alanson and ask for the money. No need to put your John Henry on the amount. Tell her Mr. Mannie says it's OK.' " Mr. Hartwick reached into his pocket and brought out a wad of bills. "Borrowed three thousand dollars from Sweetie-Pie just before she left for her vacation Friday. Bought two secondhand cars by noon and put an ad in the paper Saturday with my neighbor's phone number—he has a big parking lot and offered to let me use it. Sold both cars Sunday!"

"That's great!" Mannie said.

"Here," Mr. Hartwick went on, licking his thumb and

counting out the money, "your three thousand dollars, Mannie, the money I borrowed. And," he fished deep in his pocket, "another hundred dollars—half of my profit." He seemed to remember something, and added finally, "Sorry I rushed out of the office without leaving a message."

But Mannie wouldn't accept the money. Bulldog Drummond had his reputation to consider.

IX

ONCE A LADY
ALWAYS ...

MANNIE WAS a Victorian gentleman of the nineties. Born and reared in a conservative, well-to-do German family, he believed in the gulf that yawned between ladies—the women of his family—and those whose virtue was somewhat easier. To Mannie, the women in his home were untouchable. I don't think it was hard on Renée. She preferred to remain untouched.

My first opportunity of judging Mannie's uncompromising attitude toward me came at a wedding. I was flower girl, and the best man, full of champagne, kissed me rather ostentatiously. Mannie tore me from his embrace and almost broke up the festivities with the shouted warning, "I'll kill any man who touches my daughter!"

That the best man was a healthy six-footer and towered over my father, in no way cast doubt in my mind that Mannie would slay him right there in front of the lily-banked altar. Evidently the befuddled best man got the same impression. As I remember, he reached for the nearest glass of champagne and turned a white-livered back on my father.

When I burned with desire to enter coeducational Lowell High School the following fall, I could hardly expect Mannie to further my cause. How would I escape the refined torture of an exclusive private school for young ladies that Renée had in mind?

That I was young to enter high school was not because I was smart. Hadn't I overheard Aunt May say, as I walked out on the tennis court of the California Club, "Ruth is well developed for her years, but she's immature." I didn't exactly know what she meant, but I suspected that though I had a good backhand, I was short on mental muscles.

This was through no fault of Renée's. With her devotion to the intellectual, she put me through a series of calisthenics for the mind—lessons in Italian, German, diction, and piano— that were like the forced feeding of a goose. Travel was considered part of my education, so before I could even try for honorary promotion at public grammar school, I'd been toured through Normandy, hiked up the Pyrenees, and suspended over the Alps, all of which earned me redoubled private tutoring as a welcome-home gift.

Now there was a war on, and despite Renée's will to go to faraway places, even she couldn't influence President Wilson to grant her a passport. I was all for our president. Surely now I could go to public school. By that I meant Lowell High School, where Joe was already a junior. I yearned for Lowell and I yearned for what I wouldn't admit, for the boys who went there. Something inside my body, and also outside, had begun to bud. The outside part I might not have noticed had I not gone swimming with Joe one Saturday at Sutro Baths, the big saltwater indoor plunge near the Cliff House.

At the entrance desk we paid our quarters, then separated for the ladies' and men's sections. The attendant issued me a brass key to one of the five-hundred cubicle dressing rooms, a gray cap, an Annette Kellerman black bathing suit, and a small Turkish towel with Sutro Baths stamped in red letters on it. Along the damp smelly matting I ran to meet Joe as he emerged from the men's side. His disapproving glance convinced me that I should have brought the small towel to cover my knees.

Maybe I was wrong, for he didn't say anything about my appearance. Instead he said, "Bet you don't dare go in the deep end!"

"I know this bathing cap isn't exactly becoming," I answered. "Of course I'll go in the deep end."

Joe made no comment. He wasn't looking at the crinkly rubber cap that bulged over my curly hair. He stared at a spot right below my neck. I looked quickly down. Could there be a rip in my suit? No, all the wool was tightly knit into a solid scratchy mass.

We spent an hour in the steamy plunge with its glassed-in, vaulted roof and slush-green water in six tanks, each at a different temperature. Joe amused himself by splashing my eyes with salt water and ducking me under for good measure. The more he tormented me, the more stoically I bit my lips. Perhaps in his admiration for my bravery Joe would forget his scorn for my appearance.

It was just chance, once we were home, or maybe because my brother didn't bother to lower his voice, that I heard him ask Renée in the library next to my bedroom, "Can't you do something about Ruth? She should wear one of those 'brazures' or thingamajigs the other girls use."

So that's why he had stared. I went over to the mirror above my bureau and pulled off my middy blouse. Horrible! I was really popping. I took my black middy tie and knotted it as tightly as I could over my offending breasts. Then I slipped my middy back on. All through dinner I sat hunched over my food.

Although Renée kept repeating, "Sit up straight," and Mannie asked me if I had lumbago, I kept stubbornly bent over my plate.

Dad was the first to notice. "What's the matter, Peanuts?" he asked.

And although it had nothing to do with the case at the moment, I blurted, "Can I go to Lowell High?"

Joe immediately yelled, "I don't want to be bothered with a kid sister at my school."

Mother said, "You only have one sister. You should be kind to her. Some day you'll realize how important it is to have a sister."

Joe grimaced at me, then smiled at Renée. "That's not the real reason," Brother Rat went on. "I don't think it's nice for Ruth to go to Lowell. Private schools give a girl more training, more refinement."

Dad, who seldom reproached either one of us, said, "Professor Wisenheimer, it's not up to you to make the decision."

Would Mannie help me go to Lowell? In the excitement of the hope, I jerked up straight. The sudden movement burst the knot under my middy, releasing two small peaks. I quivered and they quivered with me in shame and anger. "I'll not go to private school. I'll starve myself."

I jumped up from the table, overturning a water glass.

"I'll die first before I go to private school. And I'm sick of all this talk about refinement. I want to be vulgar, vulgar, do you hear?" Sobs choked me from going on.

My stomach hurt and I'd hardly eaten. I ran up to my room and threw myself on the bed.

There was silence. The tears of self-pity streamed down my face. No one loved me. No one even cared. What Joe had told me must be true. I was Rabinowitz Finkelstein, an adopted child. Five minutes must have passed when the door opened. It was Renée. I thought she would be angry, but her smile was warm.

She said in a gentle voice, "Your daddy thinks you are growing up. That's not always easy."

Her tenderness made me cry harder. I wrenched away from her arms. Mother waited on the edge of my bed for my tears to subside.

She left the room and came back a few moments later with a hot-water bag for my stomach and an aspirin for my head. She seated herself once more on my bed and, without any embarrassment or detours into the private life of plants and insects, explained about being a female to me. "I'd have spoken before," she said, "only I didn't expect this to happen so soon. You should be very proud," she added when she'd finished her direct talk. "Always come to me if there's something you don't understand."

I loved her for it and I would have done whatever she asked to prove my love. Except one thing. I wouldn't go to private school.

For the first time I began to understand why my mother often said, "I call a spade a spade." Mannie preferred to joke out of a difficult explanation. Perhaps the actor is always dealing with illusions and cannot face up to life. Any family illness kindled the Spartan in Renée. Mannie not only blamed Renée for our slightest colds but fled from our bedside until the last of the sniffles had disappeared.

Later that evening Mannie came in to kiss me good night.

"Peanuts," he said, "I swung a deal. You're going to public school."

"Lowell!"

"No, Girl's High." Seeing my disappointment, he added, "Never expect too much out of life. You got half your wish. So look at the doughnut, not at the hole. Selling your mother on the idea of public school was about as hard as selling MJB coffee to the president of our leading coffee competitor."

Joseph Brandenstein residence, California and Gough streets, ca. 1901. *California Historical Society.*

Mannie's birthday party, 1898.

Looking down Market Street, after the 1906 earthquake.
MJB Company Historical Collection.

Temporary warehouse and offices after the 1906 earthquake
and fire, Spear and Mission streets. *MJB Company Historical
Collection.*

Manfred Brandenstein and Renée Roth at the time of their courtship.

Courtyard of The Palace Hotel.

Mannie's ad for coffee, 1890. *California Historical Society.*

Portrait of Joseph M. Bransten by Mary Curtis Richardson.
Collection of The Oakland Museum.

X

HATS OFF

ABOUT THE first thing I did at Girl's High was to run for freshman class president. Mannie had taught me that it paid to advertise, and persuading a girl I hardly knew to nominate me, I laid out my campaign poster. It was a large picture of a peach, with the modest slogan beneath—Pick a Peach for President.

That there were at least six other nominees, including a future beauty who seemed to have arrived already, and a girl whose logical answers assured her of becoming a lady judge (which she did), did not lessen my faith in victory. Had not my classmates, whom I had known for all of two weeks, promised to vote for me whenever I asked them?

When voting day came, our teacher, Miss Fitzgerald, waved her middle finger with its cameo ring at the class.

"And now, girls," she said in a singsong voice which kept beat with her finger, "we will vote for the president of the freshman class. Kindly raise your right hand, as I call the names."

Since the letter B was first on the list, so was I. No sooner had she called my name, then my hand shot up in the air as though a bullet had detached it from my armpit.

I glanced around at my classmates.

They sat quietly, their arms glued to their sides. Even Miss Fitzgerald's cameo-covered finger came to a sudden rest, to point directly at me. The vacuum was unbearable. At last the teacher, with her ice-blue eyes, questioned in half-mockery, "How about the girl who nominated Ruth Brandenstein? She is supposed to vote for her candidate."

The girl who had nominated me was Gertrude Gillicudy. Just before the voting started, she asked to be excused for a drink of water and did not return. To this day, whenever I get thirsty, the name Gertrude Gillicudy sticks in my throat.

Mother had told me that I should come to her when I had a problem. But this wasn't the kind. It was to Mannie that I confessed my defeat. As usual, he joked me out of my misery.

"Peanuts, run for everything, including a streetcar. Some day you'll catch it. Just keep running."

And Mannie was right. During sophomore year I was elected yell leader. Not as important as class president, but it gave me more chance to show off.

In 1917, Harry Lauder, who had been touring the United States to help raise war bonds, arrived in San Francisco. Mayor Rolph, the florid-faced mayor who sported a carnation in his boutonniere and who wore a derby like my dad's, was known as Sunny Jim. For this occasion the mayor planned a city-wide reception.

Mr. Lauder, after marching up Market Street accompanied by Scotch bagpipes and a procession of Highlanders in dress tartans, ended the parade at the Civic Auditorium. The public jammed the hall, eager to hear the famed entertainer sing in his rich Scottish burr:

> *It's fine to get up in the mornin'*
> *When the sun is shinin' overhead,*

It's fine to get up in the mornin'
But it's better to lie in your bed.

Mayor Rolph had reserved a section for all the public high schools, and each yell leader was expected to go down to the rostrum and lead cheers for the mayor after his introductory speech. Mannie had maneuvered a seat far forward to get a view of his daughter sharing in a moment of glory. Conscious of the importance of my first appearance before the public, I had secretly practiced the wild gyrations of the University of California yell leaders seen at a football game with Joe. No sooner did the mayor finish his speech than Girl's High was called upon to give a cheer.

With my heart beating as fast as my feet, I ran up the aisle and onto the platform, pausing only long enough to be sure that I was the center of all eyes. Dimly I saw Mannie wave a hand at me.

Remembering show business, I yelled in my most dramatic voice, "Now let's give a big cheer for Mayor Rolph. Come on everybody!" With that I leaped up, rotating my arms at the same moment. I knocked off Mayor Rolph's derby.

The mayor's ruddy face grew a bit more so, surpassed only by my own ruby color. In the roar of the cheers, I remembered only my humiliation.

Once more Mannie consoled me. "You and I are like the celluloid dolls you put in a bathtub. You can push us down but we always bob up serenely. I too," he went on, "once lost my hat." He did not elaborate. He didn't need to.

How could I forget the terrible night when I woke to hear Renée and Mannie arguing in the upstairs sitting room. Mannie's voice for once was not the excited one. Just a little fuzzy. Renée's, usually so well controlled, rose in repeated reproach.

"Manfred, how could you? *How could you?*"

Mannie mumbled, "My cocoa. My poor cocoa will catch cold."

Cocoa? When Mannie mentioned business he talked about

coffee, though once I'd heard him discussing rice with Uncle Ed over the phone. Something about the rice market going up. I'd heard him say, "OK, that's your department. Expand if you think it's best." I hadn't paid much attention, but now I was puzzled. Had MJB gone in for cocoa, too?

My mother made an effort to lower her voice. I could just make out the words. "Important merchant! A disgrace— *drunk!*"

Drunk? My father drunk? I seldom saw him take more than a few glasses of wine. Even Joe and I were allowed red wine and seltzer with our dinner. Mother believed with the French that wine was good for the digestion. There must be some mistake. Maybe I was dreaming. I grasped the bed covers. The bed was solid enough. I was awake all right.

Mannie moaned. "My cocoa," he repeated. "The rain soaked it and I'll catch pneumonia."

"Manfred, if you'd done as I told you long ago and worn a toupee, your head would have been covered."

"My head *was* covered. The wind blew my derby off. Brand new." His voice trailed into a lament. "Cost fifteen dollars."

"Too much to pay for a hat," Renée said.

Suddenly I heard a thud as if a chair had turned over. There was a moment of dreadful silence. Then, unexpectedly, Renée laughed.

Mannie shouted in anger. "Have you no pity? You viper, viper—you cold-blooded viper!"

"Manfred," I heard Renée say, "I'm not laughing at you because I think it's funny. Darling," her voice was anxious now, "are you hurt?"

Mannie belched and said, "Come in, Mannie!"

At which Renée became angry again. She accused Mannie of making a spectacle of himself—and with another woman! According to Renée, Mannie had been waltzing between tables with Mabel and kissing her in front of friends. I twisted in my bed; I really couldn't bear to hear them argue. I knew arguments led to divorce, especially when they were over women called Mabel. The thought was as cold and sharp as an ice pick.

I saw myself orphaned, older, approaching this shadowy "other woman," curious about her, asking why she had done this to my family. She was talking to me, one woman to another. But the voices in the upstairs sitting room went on and I was myself again, small, frightened, wondering how it had all come about.

Mabel, Mabel. I remembered the photograph in Dad's office—a beautiful, dark-haired lady. She must have been the woman Mannie had once coached in a club play. He loved to produce plays, dashing around, megaphone in hand, ready to interrupt a scene if it didn't suit his taste for high drama. I could see Mabel now, Mabel Gump, coming up to Mannie after the scene was over, wearing a fabulous green jade necklace.

"Mannie, if I could have you as a coach, I'd be willing to go anywhere!"

The conversation upstairs beat against my ears.

"Don't be a damn fool, Renée," Mannie said loudly. "I was only complimenting Mabel on the way she did her song number. How can you—" His voice trailed off in another burp.

I heard the door slam. I was alone, in a silence worse than the argument between that grown man and woman. They had broken up my life.

When Mannie came home that night he had no flowers for Renée. He held his head to one side, the way he did when he had a headache. Renée spoke to him in the polite tones she used to the coffee salesmen she had to entertain. At dinner, Mannie refused his usual glass of wine. Instead, he took a folded envelope from his pocket, tapped some white powder onto his tongue, and downed it with a gulp of water.

"Seidlitz powder," he murmured. "Good for a cold."

I sat there at the table, hardly touching my food. For once Renée ignored my lack of appetite. I looked at one and then the other, trying to detect in my parents' faces a break in the storm; but the time went on and now dinner was almost over. I told myself I had lived a lifetime (all of twelve years) during the meal. Life, in fact, was almost over for me; at least happiness was over. Mannie had probably already bought tickets to Paris where he would meet Mabel and coach her for a great professional stage debut. From there they would go to Rome and Berlin and London, and the audience would applaud while Mabel bowed over bouquets of roses and a green jade necklace.

I had been excused from the table and I heard Renée say something about how good it was of Mannie to make the effort to come to dinner. I saw her kiss the bald spot on top of Mannie's head. She added that she couldn't imagine why she had made such a fuss over Mabel. Could it have been, she went on, that she had been jealous? Yes, that was it!

In those few seconds my parents had done the impossible. They had magically put the fragments of my world together again. Yet I knew, as I went slowly from the room, that I would never be the same girl again. I had seen Renée and Mannie with a strange new clarity: Renée admitting to a weakness like jealousy, and Mannie no longer flawless. Mannie had transgressed, as Joe told me afterwards, by breaking the eleventh Jewish commandment—"Thou shalt not get drunk." They would always look the same to me, and I would always love them, perhaps, almost certainly, a little more than I had before the argument in the upstairs sitting room. But I could see them as more human.

I was growing up.

XI

NOT CULTURED

ONE WAY or another World War I affected all. There was a shooting in San Francisco Federal Court during a spy trial; Joe enlisted; I rolled bandages; Renée stopped mentioning culture—people sneered at German *Kultur*—and Mannie stopped talking about coffee to listen to Uncle Eddie's reports on the rice market.

To Mannie, the war meant the expansion of his rice business since Cuba, because of the submarine blockade, could no longer import from the usual sources. Rice brokers were combing every available market in an effort to supply the Cuban demands. MJB had long imported rice directly from the Orient to sell to the native Chinese and Japanese in California. Now Uncle Eddie's baby, the sleeper, was wide awake, offering the brothers an opportunity to supply Cuba and share in the tide of rising profits.

To Renée, the war was an irritation, a continual reminder of our German name, Brandenstein. She, whose French could hardly be distinguished from a Parisian's, and who burst into the language to the nearest waiter (if she could have sung, she would have burst into the *Marseillaise*), begged Mannie to neutralize the family name. This, I know, hurt my father, but under Renée's repeated prodding and her obvious unhappiness, he at last yielded. Two of his brothers, Eddie and Charlie, after much debate, did the same. For a while tempers flared between the Branstens and the Brandensteins, which only went to prove that none of them had changed. And once our new name was legalized, Renée's pleasure was so great that Mannie consoled himself with a phrase he often used: "As long as the child's happy, who cares?" Besides, the American-sounding name pleased Memère and Bon-papa, whose hatred of the Germans was once more inflamed, who waited for our troops to finish the *sale Boche* and give them back their beloved Alsace.

To Joe, war was the great opportunity. He was not particularly bothered about culture (although he did absorb just enough to qualify himself for challenging inaccuracies on the part of guides in art galleries, even the guide at the Paris Louvre). My brother understood our natural anxiety about him getting into that terrible list of battles—Mons, Cambrai, Ypres, the Somme, where the expectation of life for the infantryman was about three weeks. But he assured us he bore a charmed life. He spent this charmed existence in the Students Army Training Corps at the University of California, and on weekends came home to demonstrate the battle he was fighting on the campus. He would crouch at the foot of my bed and whisper, "This is the third line of trenches." He would inch up a little farther and in ominous tones announce, "Second line of trenches!" and then would leap from the bed with an imaginary bayonet to chase me around the room.

Until now the war for me had been a game also—a rather dull one—watched from the bleachers of high school. In sewing class I rolled bandages; in the auditorium, with a voice fortunately drowned by my classmates, I throbbed *Over There*;

and on weekends I helped sell war bonds in a booth under Uncle Sam's pointing finger.

. Through the power of the press, I was unexpectedly moved to a box seat. My picture appeared in the *San Francisco Examiner*. I was riding in a benefit horse show, and a photographer snapped me entering the ring. It was what might be called a lucky shot. My wavy hair was hidden by a tricorne; my eyes seemed oversized. Three weeks later I received a letter from a Canadian flight lieutenant, gushy and flowery enough to suit my overblown fancies. He told me I was his ideal, the girl he had dreamed someday he might meet. He was about to be shipped to France. Would I correspond with him?

I did not dare confide in my father. He still called me Peanuts and thought a girl of fifteen was still a *Backfisch*, a half-baked biscuit. Mother would not consider it dignified to correspond with a man to whom one had not been formally introduced. So that left Joe.

When I showed him the letter, his reaction was immediate—a loud guffaw!

But, I protested, what harm was there in writing a letter? A man couldn't take advantage of you with a postage stamp. Joe, never at a loss for an answer, told me, "The officer thinks you're a lot older. If you want to write, make it clear that here ends the romance. Tell him your age."

This seemed more terrifying to me than having to face an oncoming tank. "Can't you find some way of getting around telling him my *exact* age?" I asked.

Without a moment's hesitation, Joe came up with an answer. "Simple. Write," he dictated while the Waterman trembled in my hand, 'Being of an immature age, I do not think it advisable that we carry on a correspondence.' "

Joe, the coach, I thought bitterly, is making a business letter out of a love note.

"I haven't finished," Joe went on, softening a little.

"You may add, 'Nonetheless, I wish you good luck. Perhaps some day we will meet. Who knows? Sincerely, yours, etc.' "

Once I'd mailed the letter I never gave our postman a chance to ring twice. I waited for him at the door till the morning he brought me an envelope, which I immediately stuffed inside my middy and only removed in the sanctuary of my bathroom. "I cannot believe you are immature," the flight lieutenant wrote. "You must be at least seventeen or eighteen. Please keep writing. Oceans of love and a kiss on every wave." He enclosed a snapshot of himself in uniform standing next to a plane. He was even better looking than I had hoped.

With my classmates I was far from secretive and showed them the letter and picture. The vamps egged me to keep corresponding; the goody-two-shoes girls virtuously agreed with my brother. For the next few days I paraphrased Hamlet: To write or not to write? But it really wasn't a question. I'd already perfumed my note paper and filled my Waterman. Saturday I would go to my desk and put down the phrases I'd mentally written and rewritten all week.

Just as we were sitting down to dinner Friday, Joe came home to say good-bye. He'd received orders to report to Camp Zachary Taylor in Kentucky, where he was to enter Officers Candidate School. At table Mother did all the talking. Between courses Mannie alternately dabbed at his finger with New Skin and pressed a tube of menthol to each nostril. No one mentioned the word overseas.

When Joe asked me if I'd heard from Canada, I knew I could not lie to the brother who, possessed of a charmed life or not, I might never see again. Once more he gave me of his wisdom. "Always leave the party when the going is good. This guy thinks you're a fantasy, a faraway cloud. Don't spoil the illusion."

My brother must know. He was a man of the world, a man who was going to take up arms for his country. The least

I could do was to lay down my Waterman. But if Joe was good at measuring the distance between two points, he was no good at calculating the tenuous thread of romance. The faraway cloud soon disappeared from the flight lieutenant's horizon. At Christmas he sent me a card; in the spring a wedding announcement; and in less months than I cared to count, a picture of a dark-haired French girl with bangs on her forehead and a newborn infant in her arms.

Between times, my war correspondence was restricted to letters from Joe mailed from camp and shared by the family. "Hike, hike, hike with a forty-pound pack. I've trampled the bluegrass gray with my aching dogs . . . polish, polish rifle for inspection . . . pitch tent in three minutes. . . ." He, too, sent along a snapshot in a wide-brimmed campaign hat that covered his curls, but did not hide the dark smudges under his eyes.

He reappeared as suddenly as he left us. The war ended, and he came home without having left Zachary Taylor and before he could receive his commission. This made no difference to Mother, who patted his shoulders as if an eagle were on each, and hugged him as though he'd been through Château-Thierry. Mannie, using one of his favorite nicknames for my brother, welcomed, "My son John, I'm proud of you!" He gazed with admiration at a son who now was a head taller than himself.

The war was over and the peace promised to be dry. We were about to have Prohibition. We were about to give a new word, pussyfoot, to the English language, a word that San Francisco, with its reputation for the best bad things, was calculated to like the least. Hard liquor had never been of any importance to the Brandensteins. But like any other San Franciscan faced with the prospect of alcoholic drought, at least one member of the family decided to celebrate. People in other climes celebrate funerals and call them wakes. It was the funeral of John Barleycorn and what a wake!

On the last night liquor could be legally purchased, San Francisco held a farewell that outdid New Year's Eve. There was a parade up Market Street, mock hangings of John Barleycorn, spiraling serpentines, showers of confetti, and loud blares that joined the wails of the foghorns. Men and women loaded themselves and their cars with as much wine, hard liquor, and beer as could be carried. The law said no purchases might be made from the distilleries, but the police turned their backs on the crowds that streamed into Hotalings and Christian Brothers carrying empty baskets, suitcases, and pushing baby carriages without babies, only to come out again hardly able to haul their load.

Early that evening Joe took our Packard, which he drove with a start-and-stop action, and shot down the Powell Street hill to meet the fellows at the Pavo Real. I'd never been to a nightclub, but my brother had told me about the glorious creatures in sequin gowns who walked down from the stage and minced over to the tables singing, "I'm just a maiden in distress. Won't you fasten up my dress?" But that was only the beginning of the evening; the rest, Joe hinted, would be spent swigging in dives. Mannie had not questioned this. Instead he prepared a welcome home. He pinned signs all over the house. The first one, pasted on the bannister, read, "This way upstairs." The second was at the top, with a thumb pointing, "This way to your bathroom." The last was on the medicine chest, "This way to the bicarbonate of soda."

Joe made it home intact sometime in the gloomy morn of Prohibition. I didn't see him until noon. He came into the living room with a pasty face and thin smile.

I saw very little of my brother after that. He transferred to Harvard and, to a four-year seniority in age, he now added "Haaavad indifference."

In the fall of 1919 I was a senior at Girl's High and developing some resiliency. Studies were neglected in favor of tennis and dramatics. Renée was disappointed at my lack of intellectual bent, but Dad got a kick at my being given the lead in the class play. He even took time from his business to coach me.

It was strange that Mannie, who laughed at Renée's worship of culture, was the one who wanted me to go to Vassar. I had no such desire, and the thought of an eastern college was almost as dreadful a prospect as Mother's ambition for me to attend private school. This time Mannie would not listen to my pleas to enter Stanford or the University of California. I even made a compromise offer, which was Mills College for women.

Mannie used his old joke technique.

"You'll go to Vassar fat," he said, "and come out Vassar-lean."

I wanted to go to a western school with my friends. I hoped I would flunk the entrance exams, balancing my fear of disgracing Mannie with my desire to remain the "Girl of the Golden West." I decided Mannie wanted to tell everyone that he had a son at Harvard and a daughter at Vassar.

The exams were a year away, and I filled out the application blanks, forgetting Vassar in family plans for Renée and Mannie's twentieth wedding anniversary. My father suggested a big ball and my mother's intensely French money sophistication balked at the idea. She said that postwar years were no occasion for extravagance and reminded him of the starving Armenians and the poor Belgian babies. Mannie's moustache drooped. He said, "Renée, there's not enough 'sorry' to go around. But have it your own way."

He dropped the subject, but I felt there was something in the wind. He made several trips to New York, his eye on the rice market, which was climbing fast. He had one more trip to make in April, and Renée wanted to go along.

"No, Renée," Mannie said, a twinkle in his eyes. He reminded her of their old bargain. "You run your home, I'll run my business."

I knew there was more in this than met the eye. He would tell me little more than that the trip had something to do with a surprise for Renée's anniversary.

As a substitute for the anniversary ball, Renée consented to drive down to the Hotel Del Monte on the weekend before. We piled into the Packard for an eventful drive. Our chauffeur was cut out of the traffic three times by motorcycle policemen who lay unsportingly in wait behind billboards. Mannie was puzzled by this mounting score, but with our last ticket, at Salinas, the cop told him the information had been phoned along the route, like an all-points bulletin. "Look out for the big black Packard limousine that's on its way to a fire." Mannie was convinced he could argue any judge out of anything. But for once my father's psychology failed. The judge in Monterey fined him twenty dollars for each arrest. He was stuck for sixty dollars to add to the Del Monte hotel bill.

The hotel itself was plush, with red-figured carpet and damask drapes. It was frequented by guests who either came to play polo or who wore polo coats to watch the players.

One of Mannie's business friends was staying at the hotel; he was Albert Lasker, the lord of Lord and Thomas, who handled the MJB advertising account. This presented problems. Mannie plotted the MJB advertising course, and Mr. Lasker also plotted the MJB advertising course—and by a miracle they remained friends.

Mr. Lasker and his family joined us for dinner in the ornate dining room of the hotel. All I recall of the conversation is that Mr. Lasker at some point turned and looked at his daughter, a fifteen-year-old beauty, and said with a smile of pride, "Mary is going to Vassar soon."

Mannie outsmiled Mr. Lasker.

"So is my daughter, Ruth," he said.

There went the joy out of my weekend! I must, I knew,

pass the examinations. I couldn't let Mannie down.

Two nights after our return from Del Monte, we celebrated Renée and Mannie's twentieth anniversary. At last I
was to find out what his surprise was! But he kept his secret
right up to the last moment. Not until champagne had been
served and a Blum's angel food cake lit with twenty candles
did Mannie reach into his pocket and bring out a small velvet
box. He put on his French accent and, finding he was making
little headway, presented the box to Renée with a tribute to
a marvelous wife and twenty years of happiness.

Renée's fingers trembled as she opened the box and she
gasped with delight at a string of pearls on the cream satin
cushion. The pearls were so lustrous they seemed to glow
pink from within. A pear-shaped diamond clasp coruscated
with light.

"Every one is matched," Mannie said proudly. "Genuine
pearls!"

Renée protested out of habit.

"Money no object, Manfred," she said. I had rarely seen
her shed a tear but one slipped down her cheek now.

"Renée," Mannie said, twirling his moustache, "I want
you to have them. I can afford it. Business has never been
better." He took the necklace from its cushion and tried to
fasten it around his wife's neck.

We had never seen Mannie as much as hammer a nail
into a wall, let alone fasten a clasp. He fiddled clumsily with
the catch.

"I guess I'm a *Doppas*," he laughed.

Renée concealed her emotion in a sudden irritation.

"Don't use Yiddish expressions, Manfred," she said.
"Give it to me. I'll do it."

The pearls were beautiful in the box. But on Renée's
white throat they ceased to be inanimate.

"Look at yourself," Mannie said, pointing to the gilt-
framed mirror over the buffet.

As Mother raised her eyes to meet her reflection of parted dark hair above the circle of matched pearls, she made one last feeble protest. "But Manfred, these must have cost at least twenty thousand—"

Mannie did not like to discuss cost. Not even with Mother. Now he covered her mouth with a long kiss. Suddenly remembering his children at the table, he went back to his chair and laughed, "I fooled your mother. *This time* she can't return my gift. I bought the pearls wholesale from a jeweler in New York. And," he added, "worse still, they're not cultured!"

XII

BETWEEN
POKER HANDS

*I*N *THE* early twenties, my father seemed to have reached
the pinnacle of business success. Coffee sales were good,
but rice was even better. Renée had her pearls; Joe was at
Harvard; I might go to Vassar; the Germans had accepted the
peace treaty; and Alsace would soon be returned, as it were,
to Daniel and Julie Roth.

Of the many good things that came to Mannie during
those months of unbroken satisfaction for all, his election as
president of the Argonaut Club pleased him most. The club,
originally a *Verein* in Grandpa Joe's day, now occupied the
top two floors of a building on Powell near Post. In the
twenties if you belonged to the Argonaut, you belonged to
snobbish Jewish society. It was an exclusive men's club, the
members of which were mostly German Jews who considered
themselves as exclusive as the Gentiles who belonged to the
Pacific Union Club on Nob Hill.

At the Argonaut, Mannie could give expression to his
abiding passions: directing plays and playing poker.

Card games were for members only, but ladies were

sometimes invited to club shows. One of the features I was allowed to see was a full-length motion picture written and produced by Manfred Bransten, in which the swarthiest and fattest member of the club played the part of an Indian raja. He was called Abdullah Seemore; the reason for the Seemore was Abdullah's possession of a magic pair of glasses that permitted him to see through the diaphanous robes worn by the harem girls. In this same movie, my brother Joe was a Western Union messenger boy, a bitter disappointment to Mannie. Despite the hours my father spent coaching him, Joe was unable to deliver the telegram with any real drama.

Even at this exclusive club there were circles within circles. At lunch men chose their own group. One table made up of four old German bankers was called the "moneybags' table." Conversation was limited to the stock market and once in a while to rich *damphnudel* and strudel recipes. Mannie described these bearded antiques to others as *alte Kackes*, an inelegant Yiddish expression for old goats. He was extremely careful of his language when I was around; but many of his habits and expressions came back to me through aunts and friends, and I took a secret pride in knowing about his escapades.

Directly after work on Saturdays, Mannie went to the Argonaut for lunch and his poker game. Since the members were Reform Jews, who seldom went to temple except on high holy days—Rosh Hashanah and Yom Kippur—the men had no qualms about spending the Sabbath playing poker. As Mannie put it, the wives could make the Shabbat with culture. And as far as I know, my father never went to synagogue, holy days or not. Although he never admitted it to me, I suspect he avoided the services because the prayers for the dead unnerved him. He couldn't bear talk about death or cemeteries. If the subject came up, he'd garnish it with a light touch: "Bury me at the 'Home of Peace' and then go on to the movies."

Not understanding this approach, I didn't appreciate the prank he played the evening I was sixteen years old and had my first date with a college man. Paul was from Los Angeles and knew nothing about the restaurants in San Francisco. He had confided in Mannie that he wanted to escort me to the best. Mannie in turn told Paul that he would instruct our chauffeur to drive us to an exclusive place which required formal dress. Without a whisper of a smile, the puttee-clad chauffeur drove Paul in his tuxedo and me in flowing chiffon to the entrance of Halsted's Funeral Parlor. Whatever chagrin we felt at the time disappeared when we were spirited away in the car to Tait's-at-the-Beach, where we were informed that Mannie had already paid for our deluxe dinner.

Although Mannie enjoyed a gag, he was serious about poker. He prided himself on his psychology at cards. When the cards were running for him, he was what he called "infaaliaable"; when they were not, he played cautiously, bluffed only at the right moment, and waited for the tide to turn. Cool enough during the playing of a hand, he would slam down the cards when he lost and shout one of the expressions he had invented: "Go shoot yourself in the left *kitchika!*"

One Saturday he was sitting with his regular cronies when a relative stranger plopped down at the table.

"Mannie," he said, "move over."

My father gave this plump newcomer a cold stare. It was Jack Weiss, young, rich, and spoiled, who had everything, including a beautiful wife.

"Who said you could butt in?" Mannie said, studying his cards.

My father had many facets to his character, but none more interesting than the contradictions. On the one hand, he was the salesman who warmly greeted his customers and called them by their first names; on the other, he was club president going through the almost religious rites of playing poker on a Saturday afternoon. He resented the familiarity of Weiss calling him by his first name.

"Can't resist watching an old pro," the younger man said ingratiatingly.

Mannie let him stay on, partly because Weiss was a poker player and partly because the drummer in my father could not resist the brash and ready wit of his fellow member. Weiss had once explained to Mannie that he loved his red-headed wife Evelyn and he loved poker, but that he was never sure, during that first year of marriage, which he loved better.

Twice in one week, Weiss, caught in the excitement of a poker game, had been late for dinner. For a husband not to appear promptly for the dinner that a Jewish bride had prepared with her own hands was nearly as great a sin as showing up roaring drunk. She had issued an ultimatum. Dinner would be at seven o'clock sharp, and if Weiss was not flicking out his napkin, ready for the soup at that minute, his goose was really cooked.

When Weiss joined in that Saturday game he knew he had a deadline to meet, but the luck of the cards ran against him, and like Mannie, he had to wait for the tide to turn. Two *alte Kackes* sat kibitzing the game and clicking and clacking their false teeth. While the pots were being raked in—not by Mannie and Weiss—the younger man chewed his fingernails and whispered to my father, "Mannie, why don't they exchange teeth? Maybe they'd fit better."

"My name is Mr. Bransten," Mannie said coldly.

"OK, Mannie," Weiss grinned, digging an elbow into my father's ribs. "So you're a few years older than I am, but a good belly laugh equalizes the distance!"

The game went on, and Weiss glanced apprehensively at the large wall clock of the poker room. It was six-thirty.

"Got to make this the last round," he muttered, "or Jackie won't get any matzo ball soup."

"A couple more," Mannie urged. "Believe me, the law of averages will operate."

"Maybe," Jack Weiss protested halfheartedly, "but Evelyn's waiting for me.".

"So is Renée," Mannie observed, as he dealt the cards.

His theory, that if you hung on long enough the wheel of fortune would spin your way, was proved by seven-thirty, for both Mannie and Weiss were loading their pockets at that hour. They rose a little uncertainly and looked hard at one another.

"Mannie," Jack Weiss said, with his eye on the clock, "you got me into this, now you've got to get me out. You'll have to come home with me and explain to Evelyn."

"You pushed in without an invitation," Mannie reminded him. "Can I help it if you're late for dinner?"

"But—but I'm afraid of Evelyn."

My father's interest was aroused. While they were getting their hats and Mannie was setting his bowler at the right rakish angle, the older man studied the younger man's face.

"I'm going to tell you something," Mannie said when they reached the street. "You're afraid of Evelyn and you've been married less than a year. I've been married twenty and I'm *still* afraid of Renée."

"You don't say?" Weiss exclaimed, staring sharply at the president of the Argonaut Club.

Mannie nodded. If there was one thing he was sure of, it was that he could never answer the question he asked himself in his own home: "Who am *I*?" Renée ruled the home and ruled him. He could answer the question comfortably only when he was at the MJB office or at the club. He knew very well who he was away from her.

But this young man, who alternately attracted and repelled him, needed help. He was new to the game.

"Please, Mr. Bransten, come home with me and help me explain to Evelyn."

The "Mr. Bransten" did it. Mannie took Weiss by the arm.

"Well, I guess I started this, so I'd better stick with it. Come on."

Weiss lived in an apartment house on Laurel near Washington, not far from our home. Mannie hailed a taxi and together they drove to the younger man's apartment.

"She won't dare make a scene if you're with me," Weiss muttered to himself hopefully.

"Take a grip on yourself," Mannie said, "I'm in the doghouse, too. If I go up with you to explain to Evelyn, you'll have to come home with me and explain to Renée."

Dad paid the driver and asked him to wait. They went up the elevator and down the hall. Weiss's upper lip was beaded in perspiration as he inserted his key in the lock.

"Hello, honey!"

Mannie followed the young man in. The living room was empty. The dining room table was bare of dishes and silver.

"Darling, I'm home! Honey, where are you? It's Jackie boy, a little late but I've been having a business—"

His voice broke off in an unaccustomed quaver.

"Don't keep on yelling," Mannie interrupted. "Go in and find her."

Weiss entered the bedroom. The chenille bedspread lay white and virginal in frosted rebuke. He opened the bathroom door. The faucets, the soap dish, the porcelain tub, stared with a sterile gleam.

"Quit playing games, Evelyn!" Weiss called, as he opened a closet door in forlorn hope that Evelyn would spring out of the darkness with a peekaboo!

"She's not here," Mannie said, shrugging his shoulders.

"Mr. Bransten, she's left me. She's left me. What am I going to do?"

He began to circle the apartment like a dog chasing its tail. No whiff of perfume, no article out of place. He fell on his knees and clawed at the fringes of the candlewick spread to look under the bed. Shaking with emotion he rose, sank down on the spread, and covered his face with his hands.

Mannie pulled out his watch. It was almost eight o'clock.

"I don't know what you can do," Mannie said, "but I know what *I've* got to do. I've got to get home to Renée. We can't have two of us without wives."

"Don't leave me, Mr. Bransten," Weiss implored. "Mannie, you're the only friend I have. Don't leave me. I'll go mad."

"I've got to get home," my father insisted. "I can't do anything here. As it is, I've wasted half an hour."

He left unceremoniously, leaving the forgotten bridegroom alone on the double bed.

What explanation he gave Renée, I do not know. Probably he told her the story as it happened, minimizing the poker game and playing on her sympathy for the problems of a newly married couple. What is certain is that once dinner was over, Mannie hired a cab to drive him back to the Weisses' apartment. He could not let a fellow poker player down. Besides, Mannie scented a mystery. Like Bulldog Drummond, he mustn't let go until he'd found the solution.

Weiss opened the door and almost embraced Mannie, knocking off his hat. He was sure it was Evelyn returning at last.

"You're a fool," Mannie said, as he picked up his bowler and rubbed it with his sleeve. "You've been sitting here doing nothing?"

"What *can* I do?" Weiss moaned.

"I'll tell you what you can do. Bring me one of Evelyn's hats. I'll put it on and pretend I'm Evelyn."

"Are you *meshugah*?"

"No, do as I say. The prop will put me in an Evelyn mood."

Weiss stared at my father who was in deadly earnest.

Mannie removed his bowler while the young man went to Evelyn's closet.

"Mannie, Mannie! Her clothes are gone!" Weiss's voice trailed off from the bedroom in utter desolation. "Now I *know* she's gone," he wailed.

"Don't lose your head," Mannie called, following him into the bedroom. "Give me that hat."

"Oh God!" Weiss muttered in passionate entreaty. "I'll never play another game of poker if you'll only let Evelyn come home!"

"Ridiculous," Mannie said. "Don't make promises you can't keep!"

He poked his own head in the closet and pushed Weiss out of the way.

"I swear I'll—"

"That won't bring her back. You've got to use your head, man! Look! Evelyn's clothes have been pushed behind your suits. She hasn't packed up and left. All she wanted was to scare you. And she's certainly succeeded!"

"I'm sick—I feel terrible—"

"You look as gray as an *alte Kacke*," Mannie went on, moving things around in the closet. "Evelyn's hidden her hats under yours. Look at this." He reached up and brought down a velvet toque with a rose. He placed it on the top of his balding head, sat on a chair, and closed his eyes as if he were waiting for a message from the Ouija board.

Unable to control himself, Weiss laughed wildly. "Imagine my beautiful Evelyn with a moustache!"

"Stop!" Mannie commanded. "You're breaking the spell." He lit a cigarette and shut his eyes again. In a dreamy voice he began to talk. "Now that I'm Evelyn and furious at Jack, what would I do?"

Weiss was helping himself at the liquor cabinet.

"Mannie, I can't stand it—"

"Where would I go? Where would I go?" my father intoned.

"Are you getting through?"

"I've got no mother in San Francisco, so I can't go home to her. I'm a respectable woman and beautiful, too—"

"Mannie, are you getting through?"

My father was stroking the pink rose on his hat.

"I wouldn't dare go in a bar," he went on with a theatrical moan. "I don't drive a car, so I can't go downtown to a theater. I can't walk the streets all night—"

All at once Mannie flung off the toque and jumped to his feet.

"But I can and will go to a neighborhood movie!" he shouted. "Come on, we'll check the movies!"

Weiss drained his glass and sprang to Mannie's side.

"Mr. Bransten," he said, "you're a genius!"

Mannie donned his bowler and, taking Weiss by the arm, proceeded to check the neighborhood movie theaters. They fanned out, catching cabs and paying admission to a dozen episodes of *Perils of Pauline* and showings of *Orphans of the Storm*. Walking down the aisles with a flashlight and trudging up to the balconies, they peered through reflected light from the screen at the people in the audience. As movie succeeded movie, Mannie felt less certain that Bulldog Drummond's tenacity would pay off. The theaters were crowded, each one took several minutes to case, and Mannie was by no means sure they would recognize Evelyn in the dark, even if they stood at her elbow.

Mannie started to resent his poker-playing friend and to criticize himself for assuming a detective's role and kidding himself that Evelyn had not left Weiss for good. His feet ached; his shoulders sagged. Weiss, semi-hysterical, kept moaning his wife had met with an accident, perhaps been killed. Mannie was tempted to give him a handful of nickels and tell him to phone the hospitals. But the detective in my father predominated. He couldn't admit his hunch had been wrong.

They came to the Royal on Polk, and Mannie went down the aisle alone. Weiss was cowering in the lobby. They had spent all their poker winnings on cabs and admissions, and Mannie had mentally decided he would never go to a movie again. The theater was not crowded, and on the side aisle he spotted a redhead with her eyes closed. It was Evelyn. She was sound asleep.

"Evelyn," Mannie whispered, "Jack's waiting."

He shook her gently. She opened her eyes, staring at him.

"Mr. Bransten! What are you doing here?"

"It's Jack. He's been hurt."

"Hurt? My darling Jackie—hurt?"

"Not seriously," Mannie hastened to add. "Here, I'll take you to him. He's in the lobby."

But Evelyn shot from her seat and ran up the aisle to the lobby doors. Mannie hobbled after her, elbowed through a family party seeking seats, and was just in time to see Evelyn bump into her husband in the lobby.

"Evelyn, my darling!"

But the girl avoided the outstretched arms of the man who, though moist and crumpled, was able to jump wildly to his feet.

"Jack Weiss! There's absolutely nothing wrong with you. You and Mr. Bransten tricked me." Evelyn dabbed her eyes with a handkerchief. "Jack, you monster! I wasn't going to leave you, but *now* I am!"

As Weiss took a step backward, quailing, she aimed her handbag at his head. The shot went wild. Infuriated she'd missed, Evelyn rushed out the lobby and climbed into the waiting cab. With a sudden burst of speed, and without a glance at Weiss, my father dashed after her.

"Evelyn," he said, "get out and listen to me."

"I won't. You're both monsters."

Nevertheless she got out and stood at the curb glowering. Mannie motioned the driver to wait, then turned to Evelyn. He talked earnestly and rapidly before Jack could rejoin them. He told her about the poker game and their long search in a dozen movie houses. He told her she was beautiful, and too intelligent not to realize her husband had had a bad scare. He realized Jack had annoyed her several times recently by staying out and playing poker, and he probably would annoy her again; but he did love her and she could forgive him a lot if she believed that. It was Mannie's tribute to Evelyn's intelligence that swayed her far more than praise of her good looks. Her eyes had begun to soften. It was then that Weiss came up, and my father packed them both off in the cab.

Mannie stood alone on the curb for a few seconds before returning his black bowler to his head. The role of detective he had always relished. Just suppose he had not cased all those movie theaters! But he was not thinking of Bulldog Drummond. He was thinking of being in love and how long ago it was when he jumped down from the Brandenstein carriage in Golden Gate Park to bow to Julie, Renée's mother. He hailed another cab, suffused by a warm glow. Renée would want to know how things had turned out, and he would gloss over his role as detective and play up his role as Dan Cupid.

XIII

VASSAR GIRL

*I*T'S DIFFICULT to remember when I first noticed the change in Mannie, but it seemed to date from the time Renée started to dismiss the servants without hiring new ones.

"You know, Manfred," I recall her saying, "since I dismissed my last chauffeur—Clifford or George—I've had such fun riding streetcars. I've met the most delightful people."

There was something in the way Mannie said, "You're a remarkable woman," that caught my attention.

What was happening to them?

Soon after the conversation I discovered we were without the Packard. A short time later the Italian maid and the Chinese cook were gone, too. Renée insisted she liked to help Bridget, our new maid-of-all-work. Bridget, however, did not in the least appreciate this assistance. Renée, who was a walking Cordon Bleu when it came to recipes, had seldom gone into the kitchen except to see that the pots were kept gleaming. Now she spent hours with Bridget transposing French weights and measures into cubes and cups. She printed instructions on how to bake butter cookies with a dash of brandy, and leaned over Bridget while she rolled out dough for molasses chips sprinkled with walnuts chopped fine as powdered sugar. But if Renée was stubborn, so was Bridget.

The butter cookies arrived soggy with brandy, and the molasses chips were weighted down with solid walnut kernels. All of us had indigestion. While Bridget was fetching finger-bowls from the kitchen, my father gathered up the cookies, rushed to the front door, and threw them on the Pacific cable car tracks.

"About the only way to crush them," he said, winking at me.

In a way I was grateful to Bridget, for she had unconsciously given Mannie a chance to laugh. He continued to make jokes, but often they fell flat and he didn't seem to enjoy them. He seemed to have lost his bounce, to be preoccupied and far away.

When I questioned Renée, she cautioned me to be gentle with Mannie. He was having difficulties. She did not specify what the difficulties were. She didn't have to. Insulated as I was from finances, I needed no diagram to know it had to do with money. Yet this didn't trouble me half as much as the change that was taking place in my father. Having money troubles was terrible, but why didn't he spring back to his old self. Had he not told me that he and I were like billikins? You could push us down but we would bob up serenely! I remembered Vassar and the entrance exams I had suffered through some months ago. If I could pass, surely that would make him bob up and stay up.

When the envelope postmarked Poughkeepsie was handed to me, I wished I didn't have to open it. I twisted it over and over, staring at the owl, the official Vassar seal. I decided to get it over quickly, like a dose of cod liver oil, and gave the envelope such a savage rip that a card sailed out and landed face down on the carpet. I groped, eyes shut, to pick it up.

Squinting to read the first line, I saw the words, "This is to certify that Ruth Bransten has been admitted. . . ."

On the phone Mannie's voice was as bubbly as mine.

"Congratulations, Peanuts," he said. "I always knew you'd catch the streetcar."

I nursed the illusion that I had put Mannie together again. Yet after the first excitement of those days, his laughter slipped away once more. Not till Joe returned from Harvard for the summer vacation did I learn Mannie's money problems had to do with rice not coffee. "Commitments to Cuba," Joe told me in his Harvard-indifference voice.

"But Dad has nothing to do with rice," I protested. "Coffee's his department."

"When it comes to a partnership, all the partners are responsible for all the departments."

When I asked how much money was involved, Joe evaded the question by going into a long explanation about Cuba. Before the start of World War I, the British were the only big shippers of rice to Cuba. As the war progressed, British ships, blockaded by the German U-boats, were unable to make deliveries. That's when MJB and a lot of California rice importers got into the act. Since we'd always imported rice from the Orient to distribute to the native Chinese in the West, it had been easy for our company to expand and meet the ever increasing orders. Joe then went on to tell me the exact number of pounds of rice consumed per capita each year by the Cuban population.

Bored by his higher mathematics, I jumped to a simple conclusion. "If we're selling more rice, we should be making more money."

Joe looked somber. "It all depends on the price of sugar."

"Sugar?" I asked, confused.

Sugar, it seemed, was Cuba's main export, and the price was going down. If the Cubans didn't get their price for sugar, how could they pay for the rice ordered from our company? Nor were we the only ones involved. All the San Francisco rice exporters were on tenterhooks. California Street, where many of these large companies were located, was being renamed "Sick Street."

I wasn't interested in the others. I cared about Mannie. "If he loses his money," I asked, "couldn't he make it again?"

"Don't be flip." The indifference had left my brother's voice. "Mannie's worked hard all his life building a business. How can he start all over?"

"He did after the earthquake."

"That was different. He was younger then. Not that he's exactly old now. Anyhow, he couldn't blame himself for an earthquake. Guessing a rice market is a partnership gamble."

"But rice," I insisted, "is Uncle Eddie's responsibility."

"Are you trying to put the finger on Uncle Eddie? So Eddie's a hero if the rice market goes up, and he's a damn fool if it goes down. Maybe Mannie's been too busy with coffee to pay attention to rice. Besides, none of the partners objected taking their share of the profits."

"The losses. How much could they be?"

Joe shrugged. "Why don't you quit annoying me with questions and go buy yourself a *Wall Street Journal*." Suddenly he softened. "Stop bothering your curly head. It'll work out."

Joe was probably right. He almost always was. Just the same I did worry. I could see Mannie in my mind's eye; he was frailer, fading like his laughter. For the first time in my life, I looked away from the importance of *me*.

It was on the morning my brother Joe, now a senior at Harvard, met me at the Boston Back Bay station that I realized money could affect me as much as Mannie.

"How much money did you bring?" was the first question my brother asked me.

When I confessed I had only a few dollars and my return ticket to Poughkeepsie, Joe frowned. For a moment I thought he would put me right back on the train. Instead, he dug into the pocket of his raccoon coat and came up with a few greenbacks.

"Guess we can manage breakfast at the Copley-Plaza," he said magnanimously.

Two months prior to this meeting, I had appeared, or rather disappeared, at Vassar, engulfed in Renée's made-over sealskin coat and convinced I would immediately knock the freshman class for a loop. I had come from a place of middy blouses and yellow brick—a child's world—and here was a campus of mellow, ivied arches and walls, thronged by sophisticated products of elegant finishing schools clad in cashmere sweaters and tweed skirts. But I was the "Girl from the Golden West," and in shiny self-faith I never doubted I would be welcomed to the elite. In rapid succession and equally rapid rejection, I tried for the hockey team, for the leading part in the hall play, and for class cheerleader. I remained because I didn't have the nerve or the money to buy a ticket home.

In Boston for my first Harvard-Yale game, I knew I would never have made it had it not been for Barbara, my roommate. Ever since Joe had met her, he could talk of little else when he made his weekly brotherly phone calls to me—calls for which Joe insisted that I pay half.

When Joe wasn't talking about Barbara, he talked about Fitter Fitzgerald, the wonder quarterback of the 1920 Harvard team. Fitter lived right across the hall from Joe and was apparently just as dependent on my brother's unerring judgment as I. It seemed that no play was planned by this gridiron genius without secret consultation with Joe first. This was somewhat puzzling to me, since I knew Joe had never gone out for anything other than tennis in his Lowell High days in

San Francisco. I did, however, remember my father referring to him as a great Monday-morning quarterback. Perhaps that's what made him such an able strategist.

As Harvard-Yale kick-off time approached, our whole campus buzzed with anticipation. Each morning there were rushes for the mailboxes to see what promising bids had come through. I didn't have to worry because I didn't know anyone at Harvard besides Joe, and the only thing he'd asked me for was to help Barbara pack. Of course, he'd invited her to the game. As for Yale, I didn't even know who Eli was, except for a story in the dim historical past that he'd hanged his butler for leaving his service without giving notice.

Three days before the big game, the sun, in the shape of Barbara, burst right through the clouds. She slipped on the icy walk in front of our dorm, breaking her ankle just in the nick of time. That is how I happened to be in Boston, going to the Harvard-Yale game with my brother Joe.

As Joe and I walked to the hotel, I considered myself what Mother called *très chic*. For this brilliant occasion I had borrowed a tight-fitting, flaming-crimson felt, for I had been instructed by Joe that a cloche was the sophisticated college girl's badge. I couldn't understand why he should hurry me past the undergrads who started to form a line behind me shouting, "Haavard! Haaavard!"

Joe appeared relieved when we were at last partially hidden among the palms that furnished the tropical atmosphere of the Copley-Plaza dining room.

For the first time in months, I was drinking coffee that tasted as good as it smelled and eating fluffy scrambled eggs instead of the powdered variety served at college. I was tremendously impressed by such gastronomic luxury and the well-modulated Boston accents I heard all around me, and by Mme Curie and her daughter, who were seated not far from our table. Only a few weeks before, Mme Curie had given a lecture at Vassar that I had attended, so I proceeded to discuss it at length. Joe seemed duly impressed; in fact, to my alarm, he became so impressed that he suddenly suggested I go over to Mme Curie and tell her in French how much I had enjoyed her talk.

The prospect of following his suggestion practically froze me to my chair, but the more I demurred, the more Joe warmed to the idea.

"Don't you speak French fluently?" he argued. "Isn't it the courteous thing to do? Everyone appreciates praise!" He had never hesitated in such matters. Why, only a few weeks before, he had seen Al Jolson in a nightclub and had gone right up to him and said, "Hello," and Al had been delighted. "After all," Joe concluded, "a Harvard man ought to know what was the proper thing to do."

Trembling, I was about to pry myself loose from my chair when I saw a mass of brawn and muscle bearing down on us, with the maître d' running interference between the palms.

"Look!" Joe whispered reverently, "that's Fitter Fitzgerald, our wonder quarterback."

"Speak to him, Joe," I urged as the pride of the class drew near, but my brother suddenly seemed absorbed with his scrambled eggs. As I watched Fitter start to brush past our table, I must have gasped "Oh," or something, for he turned around and, spotting me and my crimson cloche for the first time, paused to look into my worshipful eyes.

"Hello, Joe," he said casually. "Watch the boys mop up today."

Joe, quick to grasp the straw of Fitter's arrested attention, rushed in with, "This is my sister, Fitter, up from Vassar for her first Harvard-Yale game."

In the humble manner of the truly great, Fitter said, "Good, I know you'll enjoy the game." As an afterthought he went on. "Be sure to watch me when I make the Statue of Liberty play." He took another long look at my widened eyes and murmured huskily, "You've got some lamps, babe—yes, some lamps!" Then he turned back to Joe. "By the way," he drawled, "why don't you come to my rooms for cocktails after the game? All the football team members will be there." He paused, like the practiced actor knowing his effect on his audience. "And," he added slowly, "bring your sister."

Joe leaned toward me to tap my arm gently. "Guess we'd better get going, Sis," he said. And now his voice sounded a little as it did when he was talking to Barbara. If I hesitated a moment before pushing back my chair, it was only because I was thinking about the Statue of Liberty play.

I don't recall whether Harvard won or lost that day. And it wasn't until I got back to Vassar that I realized I had not spoken to Mme Curie.

Well, it wasn't exactly a brilliant start, but you couldn't call it a fiasco either. I didn't have to come home from Vassar labeled a "pill," the title given the fat girls with pimples on their faces, or the thin ones with spectacles on their eyes. Once again I ate powdered scrambled eggs and the white canned cherries we called "babies' eyeballs," while I dreamed of Christmas vacation in San Francisco.

Surely Renée would be pleased with the eastern poise I tried so hard to emulate, and Mannie would be happy I'd gotten the character part of Gaffer in *The Tragedy of Nan*. It didn't bother me that Joe called it "the tragedy of Ruth." He'd come to Vassar to take in the show with Barbara.

When I appeared on stage as a bearded old man, I heard his "stage whisper" from the balcony. "That's my sister. She looks like a cross between Rip Van Winkle and Santa Claus."

What did I care? I'd be home soon. At Mendel's, a store in New York famous for their Fifth Avenue copies, I bought a blue taffeta with removable sleeves—good for day or evening. I wasn't pitching Mannie's allowance out the window. For those of us who tried to save, the slogan was, Look at Bendel's—Buy at Mendel's. This time I would dazzle San Francisco.

XIV

SHIP TO SHORE

ANNIE DID not write often. His letters were dictated and carefully worded for the stenographer's benefit. Mother wrote every day—in French. Her letters were more or less alike. "*Chérie, tout va bien.* Your daddy is taking things easy. He is so proud of you and Joe. We miss you."

Then a letter that started much the same but with a post-script. "We have moved. A house on Jackson Street with grill work and French windows. Not quite so large, but charming." That made little impression. So we'd moved. We'd always moved. Mother preferred a rented house. She wanted to be free to travel. I should have been prepared for what followed, only I kept weaving Merry Christmas plans.

For a long time after spinning the mailbox combination in Main Hall, I held Renée's open letter in my hand, unable to believe the words: "*Chérie,* the time is so short during Christmas vacation. Hardly worth the four days on the train each way. Your cousin Blanche kindly offered to let you visit her over the holidays in New York."

Cousin Blanche was Mannie's niece whom I scarcely knew. But how kind of her and how unkind of Renée! The knot that formed in my stomach moved up to my throat and began to choke me. Didn't Renée know there would be no holidays for me if I stayed in Cousin Blanche's brownstone on East Sixty-Ninth Street near Central Park? Or did Renée want to be alone with Mannie? It seemed from this great distance that my father was less free to pursue his mistress—business—and that Renée in some way wanted to make up for the lost years.

I wasn't being fair and I knew it. Just the same I avoided the thought that an East-West round trip would cost several hundred dollars.

If I dreaded my visit to New York, I am sure Cousin Blanche did not look forward to it either. She was a blonde, petite woman, absorbed in her family, a banker husband and a young son. She was as exquisite as her Louis Quinze furniture and as inflexible as the gold knobs.

She was very, very gracious to me and saw to it that, without being saddled herself, I received invitations to the coming-out parties. When I protested about a lack of escort, she said firmly, "Nonsense, Ruth. My son Lawrence will take you, and from then on you'll manage."

Somehow I survived fourteen-year-old Lawrence, New York, and the balls with one bright spot—a proposal from a Lowell High friend of my brother's, Lew Jackson, who attended Harvard Medical School. We had an understanding, only understanding was hardly the word for it. His main topic of conversation was, "Will you marry me after I graduate and finish internship?"

That was in the dim future. Right now what I longed to hear and feel, and finally did in June, was the grinding noise and jar of the extra engine being coupled to the Overland at Truckee for the pull over Donner Pass. Although I choked in the stuffy air of the wooden snow sheds, I didn't mind, for I knew that the next morning I would wake to see the pine trees and the red earth of California mountain soil.

Mother and Mr. Hartwick met me in the company car. Mannie, Renée explained, was supposed to sleep late in the mornings. Not that he was ill, but the doctor suggested he slow down a bit. She hoped I wouldn't be disappointed. Disappointed? How could I be? Wasn't this San Francisco . . . home, with the foghorns bellowing a welcome?

In the automobile Mother talked about the new house, and I paid no attention. My eyes were on the hills, and my ears listened to the cable car clangs. Mr. Hartwick, who generally chattered, was silent. He turned once to look at me right after Renée mentioned how happy my father would be to see me, and for an instant I thought Mr. Hartwick was trying to give me some kind of message. At last we stopped on a flat block of Jackson in front of a house nearly as narrow as Cousin Blanche's brownstone. There were two grilled windows on the first floor that could hardly be called French windows. The house was set back from the street, with only a few green shrubs and some straggly yellow broom for a garden.

Mother hurried me up the few steps to the front door and then the long flight to the second floor.

"Come say hello to your father."

She led me along a dark corridor to a small room with glass doors that looked like a converted dressing room. There was barely space for a bureau and the bed on which my father lay in his dressing gown, a dictionary at his feet. For a moment I thought he'd grown smaller, but when he said "Peanuts!" and hugged me so tight his moustache tickled, I was sure there had been no change. He pointed to the Century dictionary and laughed. "Studying words so I can keep up with my son at Harvard and my daughter at Vassar."

Most of that summer he spent his mornings on top of his bed. He went to the office only a few hours in the afternoons. Sometimes he neglected the office, and Mr. Hartwick drove him out to a baseball game. He no longer went to the Argonaut Club and, when I asked him about that, he told me his psychology at poker had paid off too well. None of the members wanted to take a chance at a game with him.

"Was your psychology that in-faalliaable?" I asked, and with a wink he answered, "Someday you'll find out." But when I pressed for an explanation, he merely smiled mysteriously and refused to elaborate.

"Well, you may be in-faalliaable about poker," I said, "but you were wrong about me. I didn't go to Vassar fat and come out Vassar-lean. Too much macaroni and rice."

At the mention of rice, the smile faded from his lips. Almost to himself, he said, "Too much rice for everybody. Too much for the Cubans, who can't pay for it. And too much for the exporters who never expected the overnight scenic-railway drop in the market. Business," he went on, "is like a beautiful ship. Then, without warning, when she's riding high on the waves, she hits a submerged iceberg and the water gushes in. The ship begins to flounder."

"Your ship will sail again."

"Right. Absolutely right. Only it takes time, Peanuts. Time." With an imitation of his old laugh, he went on. "I guess I'm too melodramatic. You caught me playing tee-ater!"

There was no mistaking it. Despite the laughter, he had changed. His skin had turned sallow. His eyes had lost their luster. Only his hands, finely shaped and expressive, were the same. He was not the Mannie I remembered. Like this house in comparison with our old home on Pacific Avenue, he had shrunk.

But Renée seemed to have grown taller, handsomer. She even smiled a lot with an unforced gaiety, as though it were a gift long withheld that she owed to Mannie. Nor was this her only gift. Late one morning while I sat on the corner of Mannie's bed, his Century dictionary pushed to one side, Renée came into the room and announced, "Manfred, I have a surprise for you. All these years you've been giving me the surprises. Now, it's my turn."

I stood up and looked at her, but she carried no package. She was elegant, as always, and even though she had on her last year's *tailleur*, the white scarf tied high around her imperial throat transformed the old suit into one that might have been Lanvin's latest model. She'd been walking and was a little out of breath. But then Renée never walked up and down the San Francisco hills; she took them like a cross-country runner. Now she unfastened the clasp of her calfskin bag and brought out a check. "Here," she said, handing it to my father, "this is my gift to you. And it can't be exchanged."

The pink that slowly suffused Mannie's pale face matched the color of the slip of paper in his hand. "Thirty thousand dollars! Good God, Renée, have you robbed a bank?"

Mother seldom held the center of the stage in repartee. Now, unexpectedly, she punned, "Manfred, you always admired my figure. What do you think of the figure I just gave you?"

Mannie stared at the check.

"Renée!" he exclaimed. "Did you mortgage the house? No, you couldn't have. It's rented. For heaven's sake, explain yourself!"

Renée was in no hurry to relinquish the spotlight. She feigned difficulty in untying her scarf. Once she had done so and folded it neatly, she placed it carefully on the bureau and seated herself on the bed close to Mannie. She searched her bag for the compact she seldom used.

"It's very simple, Manfred," she said. "You say I always return your gifts. And I did, once again!"

"You did what?"

"Only this time to you, who gave it to me," Renée went on. "This morning I sold my pearl necklace to Shreve's. And don't say, 'Renée, you shouldn't have done that.' You would be depriving me of my pleasure. Besides, Manfred, you know once my mind's made up, no one can change it!''

As Renée bent to kiss Mannie, I slipped out the door. There was no need to be quiet. Neither of them noticed me leave.

Only the ship, the one that meant so much to Mannie and all his brothers, did not sink. At the time, I thought it would have been better if it had. Insurance companies would have covered the loss. Had this been the theater Mannie loved, he might have explained the play. But he never stayed for the last act.

By 1921 the curtain of greenbacks rose on a spiraling scene of inflation. The boys were back from "Over, over there." They were welcomed home with parades, keys to speakeasies, and celebrations of bathtub gin. Few mentioned the search for jobs.

In New York the Ziegfeld Follies' girls, costumed in sequins and fantastic feathered headdresses, pranced and promised the golden era would last forever. Al Jolson, in black face, knelt on one knee and throbbed "Mammy," making the bald-headed row choke with the knowledge that you could have your money and your mother, too. As if that were not enough, Jolson came down the runway to plead, "Don't go away folks, I've got a million more." Million proved to be the key word to the rice importers, too. The traffic was called the dance of the millions. And while MJB waltzed with rice, the Cubans did the rumba with sugar.

As Joe had explained, ever since the British were forced to abandon their rice trade with Cuba, our company had fallen heir to a juicy share. When the war ended in 1918, the brothers were well established in this profitable market. For a while the price of rice mounted with the crest of the waves that carried the laden ships from the Orient to Cuba. Then in the fall of 1920, storm signals warned the ball was nearly over. Rice, and sugar, too, had begun to drop. Yet the Cubans, confident this was but a temporary slump, had precontracted with MJB for more than a million dollars worth of rice to be delivered in February 1921.

On the second of January that year, the bottom fell out of both the sugar and rice markets. And far from the chill fog of San Francisco, in the fetid heat of Saigon on a soupy sea, a ship was due into port on the thirty-first of the month. It was the *Cannibus*, a ship we had financed, whose only cargo was to be the rice destined for Cuba.

In the home office, the brothers, silenced by fear, watched the ticker tape plunge like a cable car plummeting downhill without any brakes. How, they wondered hopelessly, could the Cubans meet their contracts? Yet the brothers were obligated to prepay the Chinese rice exporters before being able to collect from the Cuban brokers. As usual, all large deals were handled through credit extended by the banks to MJB—credit easily made good in the past. Now, with the sudden collapse of the market, the company would be left holding the sack, or rather sacks and sacks of rice. There was but one small escape hatch. According to maritime law, if the *Cannibus* was not loaded by midnight January 31—sailing time—payment would not have to be made to the Chinese. And by loaded was meant the *entire* cargo.

The cables between the MJB office in San Francisco and our office in Saigon were kept humming in the hope that the *Cannibus*, due from another port, would by a miracle—obstacle—not arrive in time to take on its cargo, or at least too late for a total load.

Trotting up and down the dock in Saigon, our company representative sweated and scanned the ships arriving into port. Finally he hired a launch and, having equipped himself with binoculars, cruised around the harbor, silently praying that he would not be able to focus on the *Cannibus*.

On the thirtieth, he cabled jubilantly, "*Cannibus* delayed. Looks like we're out of a jam."

On the morning of the thirty-first he sent another cable. "*Cannibus* steamed into port late. No need worry. . . . Impossible to load whole cargo by midnight."

Next morning the brothers received a final cable. "Chinese hired thousands of coolies to complete job. *Cannibus* . . . entire cargo sailed dot of midnight."

That was the dot that spread into an octopus, whose tentacles began to throttle the hope, work, and profit of years. Rice, which once had been but a ripple in the business, had gradually swollen to an ocean-size roller that now threatened to engulf tea and coffee.

Cuba, because of the drop in the sugar market, was in the vise of panic. Banks were forced to close their doors to the lines of depositors who demanded American greenbacks. The Banco Nacional never opened its doors again. The docks of Havana overflowed with imports of every kind: Pianos, furniture, champagne, and iceboxes were piled higgledy-piggledy, for no one could pay for them. When the thousands of tons of rice arrived, there was no storage space left. The Cuban brokers, unwilling and unable to fulfill their contracts, refused to take deliveries and, more often than not, under cover of night, dumped sack loads into the sea. Some of the rice lay rotting in open barges exposed to the blistering sun and the unpredictable rain.

American exporters jammed the Havana hotels in an effort to save their goods. Bribery was the nocturnal weed that flourished in bars and cafes, where promises were made to any willing Cuban ear to, "Move, move the merchandise at any cost." Cemeteries were filled with a wild assortment of goods piled on top of graves, and the ghouls that robbed took Singer sewing machines, Bissell carpet sweepers, and Remington typewriters for loot. But it was rice, rice, rice, that spilled all over.

There were few newspaper accounts of the businesses snowed under by the blizzard of white grains. It was an individual story, where some companies skidded their wheels into the quagmire to be stuck there and in the end sucked under. Others got a lift with boards—matchstick ones at that—and finally pulled out. California Street, once called Sick Street, was running a death fever.

As for MJB, the partners salvaged what they could, set up a rice-cleaning plant in Havana, and sold, at a third of the cost, whatever could be saved. At one time there were forty lawsuits, costly and lengthy, which, when settled in Havana courts, returned but fractional sums to the company. For a while Uncle Henry represented us in Cuba. When he returned to San Francisco, he sighed that, for once, he agreed with the statement: "One bad settlement is better than any amount of good lawsuits." Uncle Ed watched his ever weakening baby for months, then he, too, left its side. His only parting instruction to our rice representative was, "Just do the best you can." Uncle Max went to Havana for three weeks, then came home, his round cheeks flattened, his body covered with prickly heat. Mannie never went.

Though I dimly grasped that the cash drawer was stuck, I was sure Mannie could press his finger against the spring and release it again. Shielded against realities, I had no conception of how great was the loss. The cash figures tell the story. MJB, from a steady climb in the rice trade since 1914 till it reached a peak of $15 million gross in 1919, was hurtled overnight to minus zero.

I saw Mannie only once more after I returned to Vassar. He came to New York on a quick trip to meet his rice representative from Cuba. Mannie was staying at the Pennsylvania Hotel instead of the Plaza, and I recall the long corridors with doors partitioned at the bottom so shoes could be placed there to be polished during the night. It gave me the same feeling of regimentation I had at college. He did not give me the lift I expected. I had wanted him to coach me for a part in the Third Hall play, but when I went over my lines with him in the hotel bedroom, he scarcely listened. I could sense an impatience, not with me, but to get away to meet his man from Cuba. Not till I'd twice asked, "How am I doing?" did he answer, "Great! Just great." Reaching for his derby, he added, "Can you take care of yourself this afternoon? I'll meet you at the station."

When we kissed good-bye at Grand Central and I saw him walk away, I noticed that for the first time his derby was not cocked. It was set straight on his head. Awkwardly.

The desk was a rolltop, with a lopsided chair in front of it. Mannie had sat there for many years smoking cigarettes, while the swinging pendulum of the old wall clock furnished a companionable time beat. The peeling gilt letters on the big black safe announced:

M. J. BRANDENSTEIN & COMPANY
IMPORTERS COFFEE TEA AND RICE, 1892

How many times had I sat there on the leather couch with its loose buttons, listening to Mannie's laughter? Now, the lopsided chair was gone. The desk was gone, though not before Joe had discovered a secret drawer in which was an envelope marked: "Poker winnings—for Renée." Inside was nearly twenty thousand dollars. So I had found out about Mannie's poker winnings, just as he had promised.

Business, the elusive, demanding mistress, had broken Mannie. He was enslaved by her, lavishing on her his talents, those vaudeville acts in which he wore many hats—salesman, promoter, adman. Despite her cruelty and indifference—the fire of 1906 and then the rice crash of 1920—he continued to love her right to the end, still clinging to the illusion that she would give him something in return.

When I recall our parting I wish Mannie could have lingered to see his business, like the phoenix, rise big and strong once more. But Mannie, actor that he was, for once had chosen the wrong exit line.

PART II
MARTINIS

Charlie and Ruth

XV

CHARLIE

*A*FTER MANNIE* died, I slotted into the group pattern of the twenties—nice girl from nice family marries promising young man, preferably a professional one. Nor would Renée presume to impose her loneliness on my future. "I think of Manfred every day," she told me, "but one has to adjust to life." Adjust she did. From then on until her death at ninety, she lived alone, traveled alone, and refused to remarry.

And I, as expected, conformed to the pattern and married Lew Jackson, who'd come back to San Francisco, surgeon's degree in hand and ready to hang it up on an office wall. Gradually I was to discover I could never compete with my husband's scalpel, medical tracts, and the drama of the operating room theater. In the meantime, I raised a family and saw Lew through World War II, my son through the Korean conflict, my daughters through their teens to marriageable age.

Lew was as absorbed as ever in his work, while my life

had come to a standstill. I took the plunge. Six weeks later I was "Reno-vated" and our marriage was over.

As an unhappy member of the "ex-wives league," I was sure it was all over for me, too. The odds were against me. Then, like the unpredictable turn of a card, along came Charlie.

It all began on an ordinary evening. I was sitting alone in the upstairs library trying not to feel sorry for myself when the phone rang. I picked up the receiver to hear my brother Joe ask, "How would you like to come to my home for dinner tomorrow night? Charlie McDougall will call for you. Remember Charlie?"

Immediately a scene clicked back into my mind. On a luncheon date, just before I had left for Reno, I had walked into the El Prado dining room of the old Plaza Hotel on Union Square. The Hyatt, with its look-alike dining rooms, stands in its place today. Then, though, there was a sense of privacy and an aura of elegance to the semilighted tables with their single carnation in the slim vase and the leather-cushioned booths. For admission, one had to wait behind a red velvet loop until Walter, the hard-to-please maître d', unfastened the clasp and nodded his permission.

On my way to a booth I recognized Joe seated at a table. A large man with sloping athlete's shoulders sat opposite him, a martini glass in his hand.

Joe motioned to me, and as I approached, both men rose courteously. "This is my sister, Ruth," Joe said. "Meet Charlie McDougall. He's with BBD&O. You've heard of them?"

I smiled, remembering that the initials stood for Batten, Barton, Durstine and Osborn, the national advertising agency, whose name Jack Benny once quipped sounded like a trunk falling downstairs backward.

I glanced up at Charlie. He was big all right, maybe six

feet two. He had an air of confidence, the kind you expected from an adman. Yet his eyes reminded me of a St. Bernard's. Not until later did I notice the slightly Magyar slant at the corners. He didn't give me a "Pleased to meet you." Instead he made a clucking sound, looked at the polka-dot dress I was wearing, and said, "I see spots before my eyes." The way he said it made me feel the dots were sparkling.

It must have been the first sip that did it. I didn't know at the time, of course, that my future was to be a martini, an olive, and Charlie.

Joe's voice brought me back. "Well, can you make it tomorrow?"

"Sure," I said, and when I asked whether Charlie was here on a visit, Joe answered, "No, he's moving to San Francisco," and went on to explain BBD&O's decision to open a West Coast office that Charlie and a partner were to head.

I wasn't interested in business arrangements. "Is he alone?" I asked cautiously.

"Forgot to mention, his marriage is on the rocks."

Common cause, I thought, and hung up the phone.

Two years later I married my adman—a marriage that lasted twenty years. And if the adman's image has been set in the public mind by such tales as *The Hucksters* and *The Man in the Gray Flannel Suit*, how about the man who doesn't fit the Madison Avenue picture? Or any other for that matter? Like Mannie, Charlie couldn't be pegged.

So, at last I'd found a people mixer. What I didn't suspect was that I'd tangled with a mix master. Nor did I realize, if it takes two to tangle, there's one who gets tangled. Me.

XVI

THE SHOW
IS ON THE ROAD

*A*T *MY* introduction into advertising society in the East,
I remembered the ad psychology Mannie had taught
me. I would help my husband and air the wisdom I'd
learned at my father's knee.

We went to New York in March. The wind was making a
final bluster. Inside the entrance hall of Bruce Barton's town
house, muted lights and thick carpeting denied the outer chill.

Charlie shrugged off his overcoat and handed it to the
butler, while a maid in proper black and starched apron took
my wrap. I reached for Charlie's arm and was reassured by his
approving glance at my tulle-veiled hat and cocktail satin.
Once he had guided me into the living room toward the wives'
reception line, I let go his security arm. "I don't mind intro-
ducing myself. Can see all your buddies waving at you."

Charlie gave me a grateful smile and went on his way.

With determined glitter, I edged into the tightly packed
line and gradually began to tarnish. Wives in front of me,
wives in back of me, eager as I, to worship at Bruce Barton's

shrine. When my turn came to be presented, my advance was blocked by a tawny lioness. She must be Mr. Barton's confidential secretary, who, Charlie had explained, took over social duties when Mrs. Barton was away. I looked into the appraising eyes and wished Mrs. Barton could have stayed for the party.

"I'm Charlie McDougall's wife," I said.

The lioness gave me a crisp nod and, in the tones of a countdown, announced, "Charlie McDougall's wife, Mr. Barton."

This time I looked up into intense blue eyes, softened by a crinkle of lines at the corners. I had the impression that this elegant gentleman, with curly gray hair, might have bypassed me and my tulle with a courteous bow had it not been for the name McDougall.

"So, you're Charlie's wife." He smiled as though he held a secret key to a compartment just beyond my reach.

Like a too-long-opened bottle of Canada Dry, I forced a flat bubble, "My husband has told me all about you—"

Mr. Barton cut my cliché with an easy wave. "Never mind about me. Let's talk about Charlie."

Anxious for a revelation from a man who was an authority on the Bible as well as advertising, I teetered on high heels. Did he approve of me? Would he recognize me as the little woman behind the adman's throne? What mystic thought would he pass on me?

Mr. Barton's smile changed to a chuckle. "My dear," he said, and his eyes seemed to pierce through the draped tulle of my cocktail hat right down to my inner insecurity, "don't ever try to change Charlie McDougall."

Left with this cryptic remark, I was dismissed with another curt nod from the lioness, while Mr. Barton, in quick succession, acknowledged a platinum blonde, a dowager in an inverted flower-pot hat, and a woman whose rugged features suggested she should have been carrying a machete instead of a handbag. With relief I welcomed the martini proffered by a passing waiter. As Charlie often quoted, "Candy is dandy, but liquor is quicker" (Ogden Nash). Within minutes the glow of assurance spread through me once more. After all, how could I expect strangers to single me out? Why be upset? If the mountain wouldn't come to Mohammed, then Mohammed should go to the mountain. The answer was so simple, it had eluded me. But, which mountain to choose. The room was filled with peak-sized advertising men.

In hopes of an omen, I started to sip my martini. Just then I felt a brush against my arm. A few drops from the drink spilled onto my dress and a voice apologized, "So sorry."

"It's nothing," I murmured and turned to see a small hill of a man with moss green eyes lost among the surrounding peaks.

About to raise my glass once more, I paused, realizing I'd indeed been given a sign. This little hill could be none other than lil' ole' Alex Osborn. According to Charlie, Alex was the Norman Vincent Peale of the firm—the inspiration man who combined ideas with ideals.

In a wave of euphoria I gushed, "I'm Ruth McDougall, Charlie's wife. You must be the genius who dreams up campaigns."

"Dreams?" he said with a thin smile. "I guess your husband told you that gag."

Behind me I heard someone guffaw.

What gag? What had I said that was so funny?

Not till later did I discover that the small man was not lil' ole' Alex. He was the account executive for Modess. As the story went, he was trying to figure a slogan for this delicate account but could come up with nothing appropriate. Over and over he wrote "Modess . . . Because." Finally he'd fallen asleep. At BBD&O this was called the Sleeper Campaign.

Now he excused himself and disappeared amongst the

cocktail swingers. Baffled again, I helped myself to an hors d'oeuvre and joined a group around the piano, where a man who looked Boston proper sat at the keyboard and sang, "If you want to keep your privates cool, send them to a private school."

So this was Madison Avenue *sous cloche*! I was becoming increasingly confused, but I wouldn't run like a forlorn puppy to Charlie for refuge. I couldn't have if I tried, for no sooner did I spot him by a paneled wall than he vanished to reappear by a stained-glass window, always surrounded by what appeared to be a football huddle. Above the party's yak, yak, the "Hi, Mac" and the "Long time no see, Mac" drifted my way. Like England, the sun never set on Charlie's territory. This was his world, or at least a big part of it. And corny as it may sound, I'd assumed when I married him he'd be mine, if not alone, at least I would be the hub of the wheel around which he revolved. Now, I felt like a dot on the circumference. Not that he ignored me. Every now and again he'd break through his magic circle, gather me out of a corner, and force a gap into the group. He pelted names at me: "Tom Dillon, bet you never knew he was once a gripman on the San Francisco cable car; Ben Duffy, started as an errand boy for the company and worked his way to the top; Charlie Brower, the great headline man." Always Charlie ended his introductions with "Meet my wife, Ruth. Isn't she charming?" No sooner had I received the polite nods than the circle closed once more to leave me on the rim.

The party broke up around midnight. By then I was not only dizzy from extra martinis, but also a candidate for starving Armenia. Back in our hotel room, Charlie bedazzled me with his smile. As I untwisted my veil he said without looking at me, "That hat is so becoming," and then rushed, "Wasn't it great? Isn't Bruce Barton handsome? You know he was known as the best-dressed man in Washington." Not pausing for a response, he went on. "Did I ever tell you the story about Bruce when he was in Congress? He was made the head of Indian Affairs. Rube Goldberg sent a telegram congratulating him, 'Sorry I've never had an affair with an Indian.' "

In appreciation of the joke, my stomach rumbled.

"What did you say?" Charlie asked.

Without knowledge of future slogans, I answered, "I can't believe I drank the whole thing."

"Didn't you enjoy yourself?"

"Sure, sure, I felt like the little girl who came home from the birthday party and when her mother asked, 'What did our little girl do at the party?' she answered, 'I throwed up.' "

Charlie's eyes widened. "What's wrong?"

"What's right? Everybody knows you. *Nobody* knows me. Besides I'm hungry. Damn hungry. Caviar and pâté are great for openers. What's for fillers?"

Charlie, already in his pajamas, flopped onto the bed. "Darling, everybody loved you." He yawned. "If you're hungry, I'll send for a sandwich."

"Forget the sandwich. I couldn't eat a mouthful I'm choked up with so much goodwill." Holding my pounding head with one hand, I grabbed a nightgown out of the dresser drawer with the other. Then, ashamed my jealousy was showing, I leaned to kiss him.

He was snoring. I clicked off the bedside lamp, said good night to myself and, half punchy, fell asleep. Not for long. Suddenly the lamp was switched on again. Charlie, eyes firmly closed, was sitting bolt upright in bed. He waved a beckoning hand into space. "Waiter, waiter," he called, "bring me a double martini. And"—he pointed to me—"bring Mrs. McDougall over here, seventeen brownies."

Had I married an adman or a madman? I reached over and shook his shoulder. With a beatific smile, he sank back against the pillows and into oblivion. I switched off the light, consoling myself that although Charlie might not have known what he said, at least he was subconsciously thinking of me.

XVII

THREE MUSCATEL-EERS

WE WERE well on our way from the East to the West Coast, and I was not so well on my way to recovery from Charlie's "great society" of friends, when suddenly I had an inspiration on how to pump up my deflated ego.

"We've a few extra days left before you have to be back in the saddle. Let's get off the train at Reno, hire a drive-yourself, and stop off at Lake Tahoe. You've never seen my little cabin in the pines."

Charlie, with the euphoria of the newlywed, gave me a whatever-you-say nod. Immediately I felt revitalized. Tahoe was *my* territory, *my* land, my chance to introduce Charlie to all the people I'd known at the lake for the past fifteen years. I'd had the "Meet my wife. Isn't she charming?" bit long enough. Now it would be "Meet my husband."

Why, I knew Tahoe back in the days when Cal-Neva Lodge was the only gambling casino at the north end of the lake; knew the owners Graham and McKay before they were sent to Folsom prison for having hidden out Baby Face Nelson; knew it before it was destroyed by fire. Now there was a new plush Cal-Neva and a series of less colorful owners. The only landmark of the old lodge was the chalked line dividing the floor between California and Nevada; on one side the diners laid their money on the white tablecloths and on the other laid their money on the green baize of the gaming tables. It had become touristy. Nowadays, those in the know, I bragged to Charlie, went to the North Shore Club, perched high on a cliff on the Nevada side.

While winding up Mt. Rose in the drive-yourself, I hid my cunning under an outpour of enthusiasm. Lake Tahoe, I told him, was the eighth wonder of the world, the turquoise bowl of the Sierra. He'd love the sandy beach and the cabin, whose knotty-pine walls reminded me of slats of an orange crate. "Wait," I rattled on, "till we go to the North Shore Club gambling tonight." I knew the owner, Luckie Harris, who treated me to drinks, sending them over while I played roulette, so I wouldn't have to leave the table.

"Look," I said when we reached Mt. Rose summit and caught the first glimpse of blue-green water through the pines. "Isn't the lake gorgeous?"

For a moment Charlie stared at the once white snow melting now into brown splotches on the ground. He took a deep breath. Was it the seven-thousand-foot altitude, or had I become too lyrical? For a while I stopped with the descriptions.

In silence we drove down to the base of the mountain and along the rim of the lake. Before we crossed under a banner announcing You Are Entering California, Charlie inhaled deeply once more. "Luckie Harris, did you say? Sounds like a good Joe. Where's the North Shore Club?"

"We just passed it." I turned to nod toward a large white building whose neon lights were dimmed by the sparkle of noonday sun.

"Why don't we stop off for a freshener?"

Hot and sticky, I was anxious to get to the cabin, un-pack, and flip into the cold lake water. About to say so, I stopped myself. After all it was my turn to be gracious. "OK. Only let's cut it short. We'll have plenty of time tonight."

Charlie turned the car around and drove into the North Shore Club parking lot. Together we climbed the steps and entered the casino, to be greeted by the slam bang and the perpetual motion of the slot machines.

Luckie, positioned near the bar and keeping a split-eye watch on the customers at the gambling tables and those en-tering the casino, waved a hand in recognition. I rushed to-ward him while Charlie, towering behind, followed. "Luckie," I said, "meet my husband, Charlie McDougall." With diffi-culty I restrained myself from adding, "Isn't he charming?"

Luckie's smile cut into the scar on his left cheek. He extended a hand to Charlie. "Haven't I seen you some place? Chicago, maybe?"

"Could be. Knew the Wertheimer boys back there."

The Wertheimers! The Purple Gang! Did Charlie know them, too?

"How about that," Buckie said. "I ran the Dunes for them in Palm Springs till California cracked down on gam-bling."

Faster than a croupier can say seven away, the two shift-ed me out of their conversation, and I, tired of being the little woman who wasn't there, kneaded Charlie's arm and in voice loud and clear said, "We'll be back this evening, Luckie. First, got to show my husband the mountain cabin."

"Sure, sure." Luckie looked past me at the gaming tables, then settled his gaze on Charlie again. "I'll save you a table by the window." And, he added, "Dinner is on me."

So this was my land! After fifteen years, Luckie treated me to drinks. After fifteen minutes, Charlie got the free-dinner award.

On our way out of the casino, Charlie waved jauntily to one of the ever-present security officers. "See you later," Charlie said.

The guard, as if he'd been addressed by a commanding officer, snapped to attention. "My pleasure, sir," he beamed.

No stony-faced guard had ever smiled at me.

I suppressed my momentary twinge of jealousy and hurried to the car, anxious to show Charlie the cabin. We passed Kings Beach with its gimcracker tourist shops and the Buckhorn Tavern, turned off the highway and down a narrow road. "Stop," I said, "this is it."

Partially hidden by one lone pine could be seen the log sides of a cabin and the brick chimney outlined against the sky. I ran up the rickety boardwalk, found the house key hidden behind a pine cone on a windowsill, and opened the front door. "Welcome to our little nest in the West."

Back of me Charlie lugged the suitcases. With a huff and a puff he set them down on the bare wooden floor of the living room. Then he sank down on a rattan chair and let out a "Whew!"

"You like it?" I asked.

He made no answer. He was coughing into his handkerchief.

"Darling," I said, "it's the altitude. Rest a moment. We'll unpack later. I'll just get out my bathing suit and lay out your trunks." I went into the bedroom to change. When I came out, Charlie had put away his handkerchief and taken off his shoes. He was massaging his feet. "They swell in the heat."

"The cool water will shrink them back to size. You haven't lived till you've taken a swim in the lake."

With a sigh Charlie pushed out of the chair and started for the bedroom. Halfway there he screamed, "Ouch!"

"Now what's wrong?"

"Got a splinter right through my sock."

"Oh, I'll get a needle."

Charlie waved me aside. "I'm OK. I'll be right out."

A few minutes later he reappeared in his trunks, marble white, a twist of Christian-martyr smile on his lips.

"Come on," I said and led the way across the porch and over the burning sand to the water's edge. Charlie followed my trail with a hop, skip, and jump, dipped one toe into the icy water, and retreated with an unsuppressed moan. "Darling, I prefer the Frigidaire. Amuse yourself. I'll go pick up some groceries."

I called after him, "We don't need much. Remember, Luckie's buying dinner. And tomorrow we leave for San Francisco."

Charlie did not bother to turn his head. His only acknowledgement was the rev of the drive-yourself motor. Purposely punishing myself for being a nagging wife, I plunged into the ice-cube water. After avoiding a school of minnows and cutting my foot on a sharp rock, I stretched out on a bath towel and let the sun do its healing.

About a half hour later, I heard the crunch of car wheels coming to a halt, followed by two sharp raps on the front door. Damn! Why hadn't I told Charlie to come around the beach side? Irritated, I shouted, "Coming!" and without bothering to pull up my bathing suit straps, hotfooted it over the sand, up the porch steps, and into the living room. Groggy from the sun, I opened the front door and for a moment thought Charlie had turned into triplets. Gradually coming into focus, the blur cleared. Before me stood three giants, all wearing ten-gallon hats and with faces Wilkinson's sword blades had never desecrated.

The biggest bluebeard cocked his hat and demanded, "Where's Charlie?"

I adjusted the slipped straps of my bathing suit. "You mean *Mr.* McDougall."

"Yeah, guess that's right. Where is he?"

The straps began to slip again. Also my dignity. "I don't know."

The other two bluebeards stared at my legs while their spokesman went on. "He said he'd find us guard jobs at the North Shore. Said he'd fix it up with Luckie Harris."

I stifled my amazement. Guards! They looked more like fugitives from a chain gang. But lest I antagonize them, I trembled a smile. "If Mr. McDougall told you so, I suppose he meant it. And now," I said edging away, "if you will excuse me, I have a date with the sun."

As if on signal, all three swept off their hats, turned on their boots, and plunked down the boardwalk.

When Charlie finally reappeared around sunset, his face was concealed behind a couple of bags brimming with groceries. At the sight of the overload, I almost forgot the three muscatel-eers. I followed him into the kitchen and watched him deposit prize after prize onto the table—a Westphalian ham, a tin of caviar, a bottle of sparkling Burgundy. "How," I asked, trying to keep a thin line of understanding in my voice, "can we possibly use all that? We're going out for dinner and we leave for San Francisco tomorrow."

Charlie shrugged. "We can always take what we don't need home with us."

I might have said no more if he hadn't pulled out a large round of Camembert cheese. "That's going to smell just great when we drive through Sacramento tomorrow. I hear it was 110 degrees there today. Oh," I went on, "which reminds me, you had three stinky callers this afternoon. Where did you meet those gangsters?"

Charlie's eyes turned from St. Bernard to Newfoundland. "They told me they are Texas Rangers."

I started to laugh. "Are you sure they're not Canadian Mounties?" Once more I asked, "Where did you meet them?"

Well, Charlie explained, it was hot, he'd stopped at the Buckhorn for a beer, and—

I didn't let him go on. I guessed the rest. In a moment of largesse, and in the dim lights and with his faith in mankind, he'd listened to their hard-luck story of no funds and suggested they get jobs as guards at the North Shore Club. "How could you?" I demanded.

"Let's forget it," Charlie said. "They probably have."

Well, if he could be so nonchalant, why shouldn't I? It was time for me to change from my wet bathing suit and prepare for evening sports. Off and running an hour later, we drove along the road, inhaling the witch hazel scent of the pines. At the North Shore Club, already jammed with Saturday night vacationers, the air—what was left of it—was laden with smoke and laced with the aroma of alcohol.

Luckie, with his ever-casing eye, noted our entrance. With a wave at Charlie, he maneuvered us through the crowd and led us to a table by the window with a view of the moon, stars, and silver-streaked lake. Some enchanted evening! My hope was, that across the crowded room, I wouldn't meet a bluebeard stranger. To my relief there was not one in sight.

No sooner had Charlie finished his Caesar salad and marbled steak, than he got up and walked into the gaming room. So what? The deluxe dinner was on Luckie. I pushed my plate aside and followed. Charlie was already at the crap table, shaking a pair of dice high in the air. I wasn't going to cramp his style. Besides, I belonged to the penny ante group. I found a spot at the roulette table where I could make my five dollars, at twenty-five cents a bet, keep me from going into hock.

I'd lost about a dollar when I heard the page. "Charlie McDougall. Charlie McDougall. Telephone."

I looked over at the crap table where Charlie, unconcerned, motioned to the croupier to cash a check. I hesitated to interfere if luck was running against him. Yet at the repeated call of Charlie McDougall, I decided luck or no luck I'd better get a hold of him. I shoved through the ring of spectators and players, just as Charlie, his stack of chips replenished, placed a double row of one dollar blues onto the baize. Someone yelled, "Eleven dice!" and let out a cheer while Charlie raked in a leaning tower of chips. They spilled his way as I nudged him. "You're wanted on the phone."

Without turning his head, he said, "You answer it."

About to reach the phone booth, I was intercepted by Luckie. "Never mind. I took care of it."

"What?"

"Don't ask questions. Get your husband out of here. Pronto."

"I don't get it. Why?"

Luckie shook his head. "You're wasting time. But I'll give it to you fast. Three bums came here this afternoon and said Charlie would see they got jobs as guards." Luckie's scar creased in a twisted smile. "Little lady, I like your husband. But I don't want no tramps in here. I gave them the bum's rush."

"Why should Charlie leave?"

"You asked for it. I'll answer. The leader of the band was on the phone. He says he's going to kill Charlie."

"You must be kidding."

"Lady, in my business, I don't make jokes. Get him out of here." Luckie's eyes were as hard as pebbles.

Alarmed, I ran into the gaming room and pushed through the line around the crap table. I grabbed Charlie's arm. "Come on, you've got to get out of here."

Charlie pulled his arm away. "I've just recouped all my losses. Going to make a few extra bets and cash in my chips."

"Never mind that. Leave before *you* get cashed in."

Charlie stared at me as if I'd lost my marbles, and started to place some chips on the line. With the strength of desperation, I jostled him away from the table and toward the entrance.

"What's all the shouting for? Don't you want a nightcap?"

Maddened by his cool, I shouted, "Don't you want to know who was calling?"

Charlie shrugged. "I can guess. Some guy who spotted me; an ad buddy from New York or Chi—"

"A pal of yours all right. The leader of the bluebeards.

He's furious because Luckie wouldn't give him and his side-kicks jobs."

"Guess they're disappointed."

"Disappointed! He says they're going to *kill* you."

Charlie gave me an indulgent smile. "No one's going to kill McDougall."

There was no time to reason why. At my repeated insistence, Charlie got into the car, and I drove full speed ahead to the cabin. Once there, I ran up the boardwalk while Charlie followed at a leisurely pace.

"Hurry," I said, as he fumbled the key in the lock, "I'm so worried."

"Never say worry," Charlie corrected. "You can say *concerned* but not worried."

A fine time for philosophy. I slammed the door shut. "Thank God we're home."

"It's a beautiful night," Charlie said. "Let's sit on the porch."

"Charlie," I shouted, "don't you realize those Texans are anything but rangers? They're out to get you."

"OK, if you insist." He went over to the fireplace and picked up the poker, then walked out to the porch and, seating himself on a hammock, tapped the poker rhythmically against the pine boards. "Let 'em come. I'm ready."

I ran after him. "Maybe you're ready, but I'm not. Please, please," I begged, "let's go into the bedroom and lock the door."

Charlie gave a last tap at the porch floor while the hammock swayed and, with a what-are-you-concerned-about look, got up and followed me into our room. He still clutched the poker.

Inside we both sat on the edge of the bed. I waited. I don't think Charlie did. He just metronomically swung the poker back and forth through the air while repeating, "No one is going to kill McDougall."

My nerves vibrated with every swish of the poker. "Darling," I announced dramatically, as the poker nearly hit my hand, "if you die, I die with you."

It must have been at that moment we heard the clacking of heels against the boardwalk.

They were coming. They would shoot my husband. I pictured myself wearing widow's weeds. The footsteps came closer. Someone was working the front-door lock.

In that instant I made my decision. The poker was poised over my head. "You," I said, "this was *your* idea. You, you die alone." I ran into the closet and shut the door.

While I quivered in the dark almost stifled by an accumulation of sweaters and ski shirts belonging to the past, I heard Charlie open the front door.

I waited for a shot.

Silence.

Charlie came back into the bedroom laughing. He opened the closet door. "You can come out now. It was only the neighbor. He came over to tell us we forgot to turn off the lawn faucet and he took care of it."

"Oh," I sobbed, throwing myself into his encompassing arms, "I'm so glad you're alive."

"Very much so." Charlie lifted my chin and planted a warm kiss on my lips.

If it hadn't been for a phone call to Charlie from Luckie early the next morning, we might never have found out what happened. The three muscatel-eers were from Texas all right— escapees from a jail there. After we'd left the casino, the three returned looking for Charlie and threatening to make trouble. Luckie and his men tied them to a pine tree and called the sheriff, who took them to the jail in Truckee.

"If you don't mind," I suggested when we left the lake on our way back to San Francisco, "let's bypass Truckee."

XVIII

I SOLD A SLOGAN

*T*HE HONEYMOON was over. We were settled in a house perched on top of a San Francisco hill, with a patio and a flower-bordered garden at the back. Settled, did I say? About as settled as anyone could be with Charlie. Recently his partner, Buck, had died, and sad as Charlie was, he now was the sole head of the West Coast office. Since coming to San Francisco, Buck had handled the business end, Charlie the creative one. Now Charlie would have to buckle down to details. I was pleased that he was the top banana. I wasn't sure he was.

Once Charlie had told me a man is as good as the woman he marries, and in my humble opinion, I considered myself eminently qualified as an adman's wife. Hadn't I received my basic training from Mannie?

I'd always had a thing about advertising, particularly slogans like Slick Chick for Schick's line of women's razors, and You *Can* Take It with You for Hertz drive-yourself. Trouble was, I'd kept all my ideas, like so many homeless children, locked within my skull. Now that I had an adman for a husband, here was my chance to open Pandora's box. He'd listen to me. He'd have to—I was his wife.

On a spring morning, I lay on a chaise in our garden watching Charlie work on his Sunday painting. He'd set up his easel on the lawn and was putting the finishing touches on a sketch of our cherry tree in blossom.

"What a perfect painting for spring," I said cannily. "It reminds me of a slogan which would be great for some spice company."

Charlie nodded and added a splash of vermillion to a leaf on his canvas.

"Here's my idea: an illustration of various seasons, with pretty girls swimming under the sun, and handsome men skiing down a slope in winter, all surrounded by a border of spice cans. The punch line would be Always in Season."

"A natural," Charlie murmured, standing back from his easel for a better view of his work.

Ignoring the absent smile on his lips, I flooded him with suggestions.

Charlie put down his brush and wiped his hands on a turpentine-soaked rag. "Have you ever thought of an ad for bread?"

"Oh, yes. The Toast of the Town. But some ad company must have stolen that right out of my head. I saw it on a billboard the very next day."

"Well, I've got one nobody has used. Try Our Bread—It's Crummy."

"Is that what you think of my ideas?"

"They're great," Charlie said, "but darling, unless I'm handling the account, no matter how clever your suggestions, I can't sell them."

"In other words, an outsider can never break into the holy of holies? Seems to me the advertising agencies are violating the antitrust act."

"Not quite. You can always send in a suggestion if you sign a release."

"What's a release?"

"Just a little paper to sign. Should the agency use your idea, you promise never to sue."

"Never? Like, living or dead?"

"That's about it. Of course, should your suggestion be used, you would be paid what was considered fair."

"Fair! What kind of deal is that? They name the price and you can't argue."

"There's a good reason. The agencies and the companies have been burned plenty. Remember the ad Be Happy Go Lucky? Can't tell you how many outsiders claimed they'd thought of it first and brought suit to prove it. You can't blame the agencies for being cautious."

For once I paid attention to him. So, OK, I'd sign a release. I had a hot idea for an insurance company. Since all children like to imitate their parents, how about a picture of a child wearing his father's shoes. The slogan could be Someday He'll be Walking in Your Shoes—Protect Him with Insurance. Before I sent this one on its way, I took the precaution to ask for the release. Instead of a release, I received an answer from the agency: "Due to our new policy, release or not, we no longer consider outside suggestions. And thank you so much for your letter. Could we interest you in a policy?" So now, even this one-sided arrangement had slammed the door in my face.

Deflated, I pushed all my unborn ideas back into mental storage. But not without protesting to Charlie. "I'd like to picket the agencies. I've thought of slogans as good as anyone else's. Why can't I break through the barricades?"

Charlie did his best to explain that slogans weren't something, like Minerva, to spring full-blown out of one's head. There was all the production, media, and promotion that paved the way.

"You're asking for the icing before the cake is in the oven."

"What's wrong with my getting some of the sugar? I thought of a good slogan for a radio commercial."

Charlie began to chuckle. "Has it ever occurred to you that the spoken word may have a different interpretation than the written one? I remember once when we were handling the Gruen watch account, we placed several radio spots during the Christmas season. The lead line was Give Your Wife a Glorious Gruen for Christmas. Looked OK on paper, but on the air the words jammed together and came out Give Your Wife a Glorious Screwin'. Not that one can't make errors with the written word, too. Once, when we had the Michawaka rubber boots account, a bright but innocent copywriter wrote the headline, Those Who Were Cautious Wore Rubbers."

By now I was laughing, too. Just the same, I still longed for my words, my thoughts, my copy, somewhere on radio, television, or a billboard.

For a while I forgot. Then one evening Charlie came into the living room with a mysterious smile on his lips. "Darling," he announced, "I've got news for you. Maybe, just maybe, you can sell an idea."

"Sit down," I said, fairly pushing him into a chair. "I'll bring you a martini. I've already chilled the glasses."

In my anxiety, I spilled his drink. He took a maddeningly slow sip.

"Tell me."

"Today at the Bohemian Club I had lunch with a Navy captain. Retired now. A terrific guy."

"Spare the details. Where do I come into the picture?"

Charlie lifted his glass once more. "Great martini mixer I have for a wife."

I had begun to chew on a fingernail. "You were saying?"

"Oh, yes, this Captain Pawling lives in Yakima, Washington, now. Very handsome fellow; looks just like an Annapolis man should. Knew him from way back."

By now my finger had begun to bleed. "And?" I prodded.

"Well, since he's retired from the Navy he's gone into the petroleum business."

"Petroleum. Big stuff?"

"Very big! He's got a fleet of trucks and he wants a good slogan he can have painted on the trucks to advertise his product."

I didn't let Charlie finish. "I've got an idea! Maybe he could use a theme like, Oil—Buried Treasure in the Soil."

"Fine, but who said anything about oil? His company manufactures a by-product of petroleum—fertilizer."

"*Manure!* You want me to think up a slogan for manure?"

"If you'll key down to an uproar, I'll tell you about it. Pawling is in competition with another oil company that also sells fertilizer, and their slogan is The Best Thing on Earth. Now what can you think up?"

Charlie had tossed me the gauntlet and, though the product was not exactly my dream of a debut into the slogan world, I couldn't resist the challenge.

Toward dawn and after a sleepless night, I shook Charlie's shoulder. "I think I've got it."

"What?" he mumbled.

"The slogan. How about Get a Load of This?"

"Great!" Charlie said, and turned over.

Maybe he hadn't heard me. But he had. He gave the slogan to the captain, who put it on all his trucks. I said *gave* because, although the captain wrote me a letter of appreciation, he never so much as sent me a courtesy load of his product. And although my slogan was being carried on fertilizer trucks throughout the Northwest, I still hadn't hit pay dirt.

"It's not the money that matters," I protested to Charlie. "It's just that being paid would take me out of the amateur class."

Charlie cupped a hand under my chin. "How about a change of scene? Let's drive down the peninsula."

On the way we stopped at Scotty Campbell's, famous for its martinis and charcoal-broiled steaks.

As we were sitting at the bar, a Mexican boy about seven years old tapped my husband on his ample leg and said, "Shoe shine, mister?" Scotty, who was tending bar, leaned toward me saying, "He's a good kid—never any trouble." Charlie had already extended his size-thirteen shoes, and the boy was polishing away.

"You do this all the time?" Charlie asked. "How about school?"

"I go to school in the day and sell papers and shine shoes at night."

"How about money?" I questioned.

"Give it to my mom. She's going to have another baby. She no like so many babies," was the prompt answer.

"Do you make much money, son?"

"Pretty good. Only I like to get more customers to help my mom."

That's when I thought of the slogan.

"Quick," I said, nudging Charlie, "lay this one out for me."

On the back of one of Scotty's round cardboard coasters, he designed in his boldest type, I Hope You Take a Shine to Me!

Then he handed it to the youngster, saying, "My wife is an advertising lady, and she thought it up."

Scotty found a pin, and I pinned it on the boy's jacket. His eyes glowed, and then he emptied his pocket, and in nickels, dimes, and pennies, offered me his night's earnings—eighty-five cents!

"No thanks," said my husband tenderly. "Keep your money and give this dollar to your mother. Tell her you made another lady very happy—a lady who has lots of babies to take care of, too!"

XIX

NEVER DESTROY
A GENEROUS IMPULSE

I AWOKE ONE morning to see an Eagle Scout standing by my bed. Not a boy in khaki with merit badges pinned across his chest, but a man in loose cashmere sweater pulled over a shirt with an open collar. The gray hair had begun to thin, but the eyes were rekindled in the belief the red carpet of the world was about to be unrolled at his feet. For a moment I was confused and wondered if the man was wearing knee pants. No, Charlie had on faded denims. In his hand he gripped a suitcase. His cheeks were flushed, and suddenly I remembered. Grove fever! It was the second week in July, the beginning of the Bohemian Club encampment.

I looked up at Charlie and forced a smile on my lips. What loyal wife dared complain about the Grove? Two weeks of isolation for the husbands; two weeks of desolation for the wives. The men, kids again, are off to the Russian River for an encampment under the protecting California redwoods and the comfort of electric blankets. Not that these luxuries were always so. The first encampment took place in the late eighties with a crude tenting in the Marin woods. After many changes of location, 160 acres (since expanded) were bought from a man named Meeker, owner of a large redwood grove, and in 1900 the present site was established. Here gather politicians, business tycoons, artists, and selected guests who, during their stay, toss problems over tired shoulders in a dream of recaptured boyhood. The list of prominent men who have attended over the years includes presidents from Theodore Roosevelt to Nixon and Ford, poets such as Kipling and George Sterling, writers Ambrose Bierce and Jack London, opera stars, and others. All are free to express their views, for the press is barred.

These are the hallowed days, the consecrated days when for two weeks women are verboten beyond the crossbarred gates of the entrance that leads to the 127 camp sites, each with its own group and its own carefree name, such as Pig n' Whistle, Jolly Corks, Toyland, and Charlie's camp, The Land of Happiness. Although females may not enter the compound during these two weeks, the males, should they feel the urge, are free to visit the hangouts in the nearby village of Monte Rio, where the usual camp followers can be found. Like signing an ad release, this too is a one-way deal. And although what happens in the village are closely guarded fraternal secrets, one story of an unhappily married couple became well publicized. For years the husband had told his wife that the encampment lasted six weeks instead of two. After his death this tale could not be kept underground. Nor could Charlie resist telling me about the aging Lothario who spent most of his time in Monte Rio. During his absence the toilet in his camp went out of order. A sign announcing this was duly hung on the door. On the night Lover Boy finally returned, however, the sign was changed from Out of Order to read Out of Ardor?

Now, Charlie leaned over to kiss me good-bye. "I'll be

thinking of you every day. Are you sure you don't mind lending me the car?"

"Of course not. I'll manage," I said, putting a lilt into my voice and wondering what had possessed me a couple of nights earlier in a burst of masochism to offer Charlie the Buick, telling him to keep it during his stay at the Grove.

"You're wonderful." Charlie rewarded me with his top public relations smile, and before I could retract, he went on. "I always say, 'never destroy a generous impulse.' "

Such appreciation was hard to come by, and as I heard him take off in the Buick, I thought I'd miss Charlie more than the car. But after fourteen days of hiking up and down the San Francisco hills, riding the buses without a seat, and getting "tired blood" as well as tired feet, I reversed the sentiment. I missed the Buick more than Charlie.

While I waited for the return of my native, I tried to picture him at the Grove. The setting was no mystery to me, for at least once a year (after the encampment) wives and friends are invited to a picnic and treated to a tour of the grounds. Giant redwoods, like stalwart guards, surround the hills above a small lake stocked with fat trout, who swim contentedly beneath the lily pads. (Only once was the tranquility of the fish disturbed. During a drought the water line lowered and beavers came out of the woods and devoured the fish. But the lake was replenished, and once again the trout laze in the water.)

The opening ceremonies would start at six o'clock with the lighting of the Lamp of Friendship, a Grecian lamp at one end of the lake in front of Haig Patigian's huge bronze sculpture of the Bohemian Owl, the symbol of the club. As darkness envelops the camp, this is followed by the Cremation of Care. A barge bearing the effigy of "care" is floated down the lake and as it reaches the owl it is set on fire. The rising flames illuminate the backdrop of trees on the hills and are greeted with shouts of glee from the audience as "care" burns on its pyre. Charlie told me how this drama was interrupted one year by two well-plastered members who thought it would be amusing to tie up the barge to its moorings. The spectators, waiting in awe, could not understand the delay, until one of the group, wise as Patigian's owl, sprinted to the far end of the lake and cut the restraining ropes.

Since Charlie's camp was called The Land of Happiness, what right had I to be unhappy? I consoled myself with his words to me, "Never destroy a generous impulse."

At last came *the* Sunday when the Buick, Charlie, and I would be reunited. Of course, that would be sometime in the late afternoon. To make the minutes click faster, I spent two hours that morning baking Charlie's favorite cheesecake, using eight packages of Philadelphia cream cheese ground to a pulp, a box of graham crackers crushed by hand, and a pint of sour cream whipped feather light. Having produced this *chef d'oeuvre*, I placed the cake, framed in a spring form, into the refrigerator to cool. I spent another hour arranging flowers around the house, then placed a bowl of chrysanthemums on the piano near the window, like the signal lamp wives light awaiting their husbands' return from sea. Only there was no port or ships for me to watch, just the steep hill and the cars in low gear puffing their way to its top. From noon on, I flicked the window curtains, making sure the yellow flowers could be seen. In between times I ran into the kitchen to check on the perfection of the cheesecake.

It must have been around four o'clock when I heard the toot of a horn. Eagerly I rushed to the window and leaned out. No, that wasn't our Buick parked against the curb, but a big dusty car with fish tails. Oh, to hell with it! Might as well go upstairs, get a book, or turn on the television, and let Charlie wait for *me*. But no sooner had I started up the first step than I heard the key turn in the lock. In walked Charlie flanked by three strangers as dusty as the car.

"Darling," Charlie said, circling me in his arms, "it's good to be home. Missed you!" And while crushing me like ice in a frappé, mumbled, "Want you to meet—"

The names escaped me, but not his final introduction. "This is my wife, Ruth. Isn't she charming?" And without waiting for their tired nods, added, "The boys drove me home from the Grove. Can you fix us all some drinks?"

"Sure," I said, "if you'll let go your stranglehold."

Charlie dropped his half nelson, and for the first time I saw his eyes: all American—red, white, and blue.

When I caught my breath I asked, "Where is our Buick?"

Charlie rubbed his cheeks. "Sure need a shave. Would you like me to get the ice?"

"Don't bother. I have it already in the bucket on the bar." Then remembering he'd sidetracked me, I addressed the three weary Bohemians. "Where is our car?"

As if I'd not asked, the first Bohemian turned his gaze on the chrysanthemums. "What beautiful flowers." The second one murmured, "Could I use your facilities?" And the third meandered over to the piano and ran his fingers over the keys.

"Where"—I tugged Charlie's sweater—"is the Buick?"

Charlie winked a streaked eye. "No drinkee, no talkee."

Frustrated, I accepted the blackmail. I poured him a martini.

"Thanks, darling." He gulped it and held out the glass. "Bartender, don't be a louse. How about another drink on the house?"

In exasperation I shouted, "What happened to our car?" By now his pals surrounded him as if to ward off an enemy attack. In unison they patted Charlie's shoulder and chorused, "You have a great husband."

"Sure. How great?"

Nor did I get an answer till the unexpected guests had been served a couple of rounds of double scotches. Then one of the braver Bohemian braves came out with the explanation. A long one at that. It had to do with George Antheil, who was at the Grove that summer. He was, the Bohemian went on, one of the first modern composers and had created a furor in Paris in the twenties with his production of the Ballet Mécanique in which he used a combination of musical instruments, airplane motors, and steam engines. Having given me this rundown, he went on to say that George Antheil was due back in Santa Barbara for a concert engagement this very Sunday. For some reason to which I paid no attention, he'd missed his plane connection. "And what do you think?" the boys chanted.

"Don't tell me." I put my fingers over my ears. Nevertheless, a voice I didn't want to hear penetrated. "Charlie loaned him the car."

Stunned, I could think of nothing better than to ask, "Why don't we all have some cheesecake?"

Evidently the word "cheese" turned Charlie's already pale bodyguards to slightly green. With rapid thank yous, they retreated through the front door. Before I could turn an accusing look on my husband he said, "Darling, you're wonderful. Do you mind if I hit the hay?" He started to climb the stairs.

"Our car!" I yelled. "When will we get it back?"

On the landing Charlie, yawning, had the audacity to say, "Don't be concerned, in a day or so."

As it turned out I was not kept in suspense for even a day or *so.* The very next morning brought a telegram from George Antheil. "Sorry to inform you, car skidded into guard rail of Santa Barbara freeway. Stop. Will pay repairs. Stop. No injury to me. Made concert on time. Great success. Stop. Thanks."

Western Union style I answered, "Great. Stop. How are we supposed to recover our wounded automobile? Stop. George forgot to mention that."

As I might have expected, Charlie found a simple solution. We flew to Santa Barbara, picked up our car, and drove it back to San Francisco. Fifteen miles outside the city, the Buick, weak from recent surgery, burst its scars. It cost us seventy-five dollars to be towed to home base. By then *I* was ready to blow a gasket. In frustration I shouted, "There are all kinds of people in this world, but you're not one of them!"

XX

NOT A DETAIL MAN

*O*NE EVENING a couple of years after the death of his partner, Charlie arrived home late. He looked fatigued, and his smile was not on the upbeat. "Stuck at the office," he apologized.

Once he'd settled into a comfortable chair, I brought him his martini, but it did not work its usual magic. Before finishing his drink, he set down his glass. "The biggest mistake I ever made was to let Bruce Barton persuade me to head the San Francisco office alone after I lost Buck." Charlie lifted his glass once more and the smile returned to his lips. Almost with relish he added, "I'm not a detail man." For a moment the words evoked a memory. Wasn't that the way Mannie had felt about the business? All the same I insisted, "Of course you are. Good as anyone else."

"Be realistic," he said.

Wasn't I? Could Charlie be dissatisfied? Surely I wasn't. If being married to Charlie wasn't exactly sailing on an even keel, there were plenty of exciting waves. We entertained visiting firemen and clients, taking them to San Francisco's gourmet restaurants—Ernie's, The Blue Fox, and the same Jack's where Mannie had taken me as a girl on my initiation into his coffee world. If I closed my eyes, I could picture him popping his derby up and down in response to the greetings of "Hello, Mannie." Only now there was no Mannie. Now I was with the martini crowd and enjoying the *spécialités de la maison*, all charged to expense accounts and accompanied by the free flow of alcohol and the hush-hush talk about ad accounts.

Not that Charlie spoke to me about his accounts, except to tell me how he'd landed Standard Oil. When he and Buck first opened the San Francisco office, the rumor around Montgomery Street was that Standard was looking for a new ad agency. The field was wide open and all the ad boys were playing the angles. Not Charlie. He preferred the straight line between two points. After thinking the matter over where, as he told me, most men think best, he scribbled an idea on a piece of toilet paper: "There's a New High Standard in Gasoline—It's the New High Standard." Then, tearing off the sheet of Zellerbach's finest tissue, he rushed over to the Russ Building and dropped it on Buck's desk. Buck, a bull of a man with a bald head, stared at the lines. "Not bad, but how in the hell do you expect to sell it? We're new out here. We haven't even got an organization plan."

"We'll have one soon. In the meantime, I'll make an appointment with Standard's ad manager at The Office." Charlie didn't wait to see Buck wipe away the beads of sweat that had begun to sprout on his shiny dome.

Ending his story with a grin, Charlie told me The Office was a bar on Montgomery Street where no respectable adman in search of an account would be found, so no one would be around to kibitz the deal. Not that Standard's ad manager signed then and there, but he bought the final drink. Six months later BBD&O got the account.

Now, when I look back on those first years of marriage,

I realize that I was on an ego trip, indulging in the role of the successful adman's wife. Like my slogans, I licked the icing on the cake. I took it for granted this was the way it was and would be for a long time. Some changes later perhaps—much later. Deliberately I ignored the small signs along the way— Charlie getting up in the middle of the night and filling the ashtray with cigarette butts, and his easel lying folded in the corner of our patio, a blank canvas leaning against it.

When the first tremor came, I hardly noticed the quiver. Casually one morning over breakfast coffee, Charlie neglected to lift his cup. Instead he looked at my robe and said, "You should always wear green. It brings out the color of your eyes."

By then I should have recognized the McDougall diversionary tactic, but flattered, I smiled. "Your necktie matches your eyes, too."

Then came the soft sellout. "Meant to tell you, we've got a new office manager. Great guy, a genius at organization."

"Wonderful." I helped myself to some cereal. "Another genius." Not until I'd poured the cream did my reflexes begin to function. I looked up at Charlie. He was grinning. A real relaxed grin.

"What about you?"

"I'm back at my old job. Head of creative art."

"Are you telling me you're no longer the boss?"

"If you want to put it that way. The way I see it, I'm free to do creative work again. The new manager will take a load of paper work off my shoulders."

Before I could absorb his change of status, Charlie pushed back his chair and went for his hat. "Got to hurry and make a couple of layouts. See you this evening."

The front door banged shut, yet not tight enough to bar his whistle.

So, Charlie was no longer top banana. He was satisfied. But how about me? I was no longer the boss's wife.

I remembered Bruce Barton's advice to me: "Don't try to mold Charlie." But all day I planned my arguments. And that evening in preparation I fixed a couple of extra-dry martinis.

No sooner had Charlie sat down in his chair than I handed him his drink. Not waiting for his first swallow, I said, "You don't appreciate yourself."

Charlie gave me an absent smile. "Where's the newspaper?"

I brought it to him. "Darling, did you hear me? I'm trying to tell you, you're selling yourself short. You're an organization man as well as an art director, you're—"

At that moment the telephone rang. I went into the hall to answer, annoyed I'd been interrupted in my sales pitch. "For you," I called. "Person to person. Chicago."

Charlie walked over and took the receiver from me while I stood by. "Hi, Mix!" he said in his upbeat voice. "Long time between drinks." After that he said very little, except for an occasional, "I get it," and a final, "I'll be in touch."

The instant he hung up I bombarded, "Who was that? What's it all about?"

I followed him back into the living room. He sat down in his chair and sipped his drink before answering, "Mix Dancer. Know him from Chicago days: an account executive."

"And?"

"How about bringing me another drink?"

"Sure," I said and brought my offering.

Charlie stared at the glass. "Mix owns his own ad agency in New York now, Dancer, Fitzgerald and Sample. Mostly radio and television."

Once more he paused. Once more I prodded. "Why is he calling you?"

"Mix plans to open an office in San Francisco."

"Where do you come in?"

Charlie picked up his drink and downed it in two swallows. "He wants me to be president of his western firm."

"President! You'd have your name in gold letters on the door!"

"Gold letters and a title aren't always what they seem." He let it go at that. As if I weren't in the room, he walked over to the window and stared at the bay. "I started with the Batten Agency," he mused, "forty years ago before the merger with BBD&O. Advertising was a simple business then, not the game it's called today."

"Forty years ago! You must have been a kid. Did your Aunt Fanny know?"

He'd told me about Aunt Fanny. She was the aunt who'd brought up Charlie and his two brothers, Walter and John, after their mother died. Poppa, who'd married at forty, was widowed at forty-six. Left with three boys, all under ten, he'd appealed to his youngest sister. Could she—would she—care for his sons? Fanny did not hesitate. She moved into the six-family flat on Green Avenue, Brooklyn, removed her velvet toque, and stabbed the hatpins into the oak frame of the mirror over the dresser. With that gesture she discarded a life of her own. Fanny had just celebrated her birthday. Her twenty-eighth.

"You haven't answered my question. Did Aunt Fanny know?"

Abruptly Charlie turned away from the window and sat down in his easy chair. "She found out after the anniversary party."

"What party? What anniversary?"

Charlie looked at me with surprise. "Haven't I ever told you about the twenty-fifth anniversary of the founding of the Batten advertising agency? I'd just landed a job with the company."

As if I'd christened him with a bottle of champagne, Charlie launched into a sea of memories.

XXI

OUR DOUBTS
ARE TRAITORS...

*A*T EXACTLY high noon back in 1916, Charlie walked through the entrance of the old Waldorf-Astoria Hotel in New York. Before entering the banquet hall, he gave a last brush of one shoe against a sock, hitched his knickers, and adjusted the home-laundered handkerchief, which jutted from the pocket of his belted jacket like a small sail of hope. Twice he circled the group of tables that filled the room till he found his place at one nearest the kitchen. At the other end of the dining hall beneath a draped American flag, the speakers' table, garlanded with red carnations and ferns, flanked the wall.

To celebrate this gala day, the whole company had been invited—from top executives to the youngest mail boy.

Before sitting down, Charlie tugged at the sleeves of his jacket as if by this gesture he could force them to cover his strong bare wrists. Then he looked at the table setting and let out a whistle. Someone turned to cluck annoyance, but seeing the grin on the boyish face, responded with a good-humored smile. Charlie was oblivious. He wanted to shout, "Good-bye, Brooklyn. Manhattan, here I come."

Beside each Lenox plate was a gold-rimmed menu at the top of which was each guest's name. But gourmet and incipient chef that Charlie was, the menu's list of oysters Rockefeller, filet mignon, and soufflé Grand Marnier did not impress him as much as the red velvet jewel box placed beside each water goblet. It contained a medallion the size of a silver dollar. One side was embossed with the likeness of Mr. George Batten, president of the company, while the other side was inscribed: " 'Our Doubts are Traitors and make us lose the good we oft might win by fearing to attempt.'—William Shakespeare, *Measure for Measure* . . . Act I, Scene IV."

Over and over Charlie fingered his medallion. Enraptured, his thoughts ballooned over the word "adman." What a great copywriter Shakespeare would have made.

The waiter nudged Charlie and proffered a bottle of champagne. Charlie shook his head and quickly shoved his knee pants beneath the damask cloth.

He concluded his story with, "I was sixteen."

Having listened without interruption, I now asked, "How did your Aunt Fanny find out about your job?"

"Aunt Fanny," Charlie said, skipping a direct answer, "was a beauty-full woman with golden hair. Not *red*. She wouldn't allow us to call it red. She was amazing, singing while she cooked and mended. She used to tell me and my brothers stories about Indians, cowboys, and settlers. Not till I grew up did I find out she'd never been west of the Hudson River. Every Tuesday, ironing day, we'd gather in the kitchen after school to listen to her tales of wild adventure." Taking a deep breath, Charlie added, "I can still smell the pleasant pungent odor of wax from the irons that were kept on the coal stove."

It was a *gemütlichkeit* household, filled throughout the week with boisterous youngsters, aunts, real and otherwise, and last-minute guests. Sundays were the only quiet days. Fanny insisted the family attend church services in the morning and listen to choir practice in the evening. Besides, the boys were expected to sandwich Sunday school in between. But holidays were fun days. At Thanksgiving and Christmas the ironing board was spread between the kitchen chairs to accommodate the overflow. After dinner Fanny led the way into the parlor, where the dust covers were removed from sofa and chairs for the occasion. Charlie or Walter would seat himself at the Mason Hamlin organ while John, the youngest, squatted on a footstool. Everyone joined in a community songfest. As a grand finale, Fanny ran to the center of the room and, with the dimple at the corner of her mouth deepening, clapped her hands for attention. While all eyes were on her, she executed three somersaults. Of course, she kept her taffeta skirt close over her high-button shoes.

On the morning of the Batten anniversary, Fanny, surrounded by the usual hubbub of the breakfast hour, kissed Charlie good-bye after asking him her daily questions: "Have you brushed your teeth, washed behind your ears, have a clean handkerchief?" She then paused and asked another one. "Why are you wearing your Sunday suit?"

"A party," Charlie replied and quickly added, "Aunt Fanny, isn't that a new shirtwaist? Beauty-full," he said, dividing the word. "Matches your golden hair." And before the smile faded from Fanny's lips, he sprinted down the hall. Fanny, still smiling, turned to the pile of breakfast dishes content Charlie was on his way to Commercial High and probably some after-school affair. Only he wasn't. Nor had he made his appearance there for the past month. Oh, he'd managed to graduate from PS 75 and he'd lasted two years at Commercial High, which was a lot of formal education for someone as informal as Charlie.

Fanny plunged her hands into the soapy water. She had a tidy future all planned for the boy. He had a good head for figures. Someday he'd be an accountant. Not that she denied he had equal talent with pen and pencil. What troubled her was that he scarcely mentioned his good grades in math, while the slightest praise from his art teacher sent him on a whistling binge.

Yet, had it not been for his Aunt Meta, secretary to Mr. Booth, the art manager of the Batten Agency, Charlie might have ended unhappily as an accountant. It was to Aunt Meta that Charlie one day showed a crumpled letter from his high school art teacher, praising his talent at drawing. Suddenly Charlie blurted, "I don't want to be an accountant."

Meta studied the eager eyes of the boy already too big to be wearing knee pants and whispered, "I'll speak to Mr. Booth."

Impatient as Charlie was, he waited all of two days before, school books slung by a strap, some sample sketches, and the letter of recommendation concealed under his sweater, he broadjumped the front steps. Sprinting down the block he tossed school books and strap behind one of those trees that grow in Brooklyn, and with invincible faith in the future, he boarded the Elevated marked Bowery. From the station, he made the remaining two miles in a jog trot to the office of the George Batten Advertising Agency on Fourth Avenue. He pushed open the office door and announced to the receptionist: "The name's Charlie, Charlie McDougall."

She answered with a smile, a smile that seemed to be directed at his knee pants. "Go right in. Mr. Booth has been expecting you."

Mr. Booth was an amiable man who looked a bit like George M. Cohan—bald at the top with a big cigar in his left hand. He gave Charlie a hearty handshake with his right, and Charlie tossed his checkered cap onto the hat rack with a bull's-eye hit.

Mr. Booth laughed. "Good shot." Taking a draw on his cigar, he added, "Meta Hammond mentioned her nephew would be paying me a visit."

Charlie hardly took time to nod before pulling from under his sweater, like the magician with the rabbit, the letter of recommendation and the sample sketches.

Mr. Booth waved his cigar. No need for proof, he said, Meta's words were sufficient. How would he like starting work today, six dollars a week? Without pausing for Charlie's grin, he led the way to the "bullpen" and introduced Charlie to the artists. No sooner had Mr. Booth left the room than Charlie rolled up his sweater sleeves and waited for orders. He expected someone to hand him a sketch pad. Instead, one of the artists came over, placed a hand on his shoulder, and said, "Boy, fill the water bowls with fresh water. And," he went on, dropping a fistful of pencils in Charlie's lap, "sharpen these."

Although he earned less than he'd made his school days with a pushcart bakery route and delivery of the Brooklyn *Chat*, the job with the Batten Company was like being paid to go to school. As he put it, "Lucky me, I was working with some of the finest commercial artists of that day. They were visualizers, men who could carry through an idea from start to finish." Yet, while Charlie's soul was being nourished, his body was not underfed. A block away from the Batten Agency on Twenty-eighth Street and Fourth Avenue was Fink's restaurant. Fink's — despite the name — was a gentleman's luncheon and dinner place. As one entered, on the right was a long mahogany bar. On the left was the free lunch counter, which could barely hold its aromatic load—hams, turkey, roast beef, beans, salads, and a row of salty dishes, smoked herring, and pickled pig knuckles. Assorted breads were heaped in baskets placed next to mounds of butter. An immense German in chef's cap with an equally immense knife stood ready to slice meat and help the customers who drifted over from the bar for what they termed "a snack."

Now Charlie's talent at math came in handy. Quickly he learned how to stretch his six dollars a week to include a bellyful. If, he figured, he took the Brooklyn El to Manhattan, which cost five cents, and then instead of spending another five cents for subway fare, he walked the couple of miles to the agency, he would save a nickel. With the nickel saved, he bought a draught of beer at Fink's that entitled him to a sweep of the free lunch counter.

Mr. Fink, the owner, a thin little man who appeared dwarfed next to his giant chef, continually cased the goings on at his restaurant. Though small in size, he had big eyes for business, and Charlie's heaped plate did not escape him. Just the same, he gave the boy a daily "Hello." He could spot a future customer. So, despite the temporary loss, he gambled on the investment. He was right. Three years later, Charlie joined the distinguished artist's table. Costs had gone up to thirty-five cents. That was 1919.

In the meantime, life at the McDougall flat on Green Avenue might have kept right on rolling, and Aunt Fanny might have continued her dream of Charlie's future as an accountant, had it not been for the evening after the anniversary party.

Fanny, after clearing the table, went down the hall to check on the boys. Walter, under a student lamp, was intent on a poem. Johnny, who shared a room with Charlie, was sound asleep, his clothes neatly piled on a chair. Charlie's knickers and shirt were dumped on the floor; his shoes stood at right angles. Fanny reached for the lamp and pulled the cord. Charlie's large form lay hulked beneath the covers. His breathing was irregular. Fanny bent to plump a pillow and caught a glimmer of silver. She reached under the pillow and pulled out what seemed to be a silver dollar. Fanny took the coin and examined it. No, this was no dollar, but some kind of medallion with a mustachioed face imprinted on it.

Charlie turned. He blinked his eyes. Aunt Fan's hair was transformed by the light into spun gold. For a moment he was only conscious of gold, then he saw the coin in her hand. He rubbed his eyes. He's not a talker. Never was. Only, as he says, "when it fits in." Now it did. Suddenly the words spilled. He wasn't at Commercial High anymore. He had a job with an advertising agency. Not an ordinary one. The greatest, the tops—the George Batten Company.

"Oh, Aunt Fan, I didn't want to fool you. Look," he said, punching the pillow, "I'll give you my salary. All of it."

"How much are you making?" she asked.

"Six dollars a week." He glanced at Fan's hair. Had it turned red? He watched while she smoothed her hands against her skirt. She did not speak. Instead she measured the broad shoulders above the bed covers, then turned to look at the knee pants spread on the floor.

"Never mind," she said, "giving me house money. Use it to buy yourself a pair of long trousers."

She started toward the door.

"Aunt Fanny," Charlie called, "you forgot something. Tuck me in."

When Charlie finished talking I went over to him and put an arm around his shoulder. "I loved hearing about your past, but how about now? Are you going to accept Mix Dancer's offer?"

He patted my hand. "Let's sleep on it."

Easy for him to say. I couldn't. Gold letters—Charles McDougall, President—illuminated my dreams.

Now when I recall what happened, it seems to me as brief and illusionary as my dream. Charlie resigned from BBD&O. For two years he was president of Dancer, Fitzgerald, and McDougall. His name was in gold letters on the door. And I was the president's wife. He even let me work in the office, writing radio copy for the Sperry breakfast-food account. I had my own desk. Then, unexpectedly, a new copywriter needed my desk. Mine was shoved into the hall. Just the same I plugged away at slogans and snappy phrases. The copy chief, a woman with cropped hair and square jaw, greeted my radio commercials with far from an enthusiastic smile. When it was OK, she grunted. If not, she tore it up. And once when I presented her with "Eat our Cereal for breakfast . . . it's a Serial to be continued each morning," she shouted, "You're lucky I don't show that junk to Charlie!"

Maybe being the boss's wife wasn't so hot after all. Nor were after-office hours any better. Night after night we talked shop. That is, I did. I tossed the ball to Charlie while he, like an indifferent tennis player, dropped my ball back into the net. Finally one night I asked, "What's the matter?" and he answered, "My foot is sore."

"You're talking in riddles. What has your foot got to do with advertising?"

For a moment he smiled to himself and then he said, "Maybe I've been putting that big foot of mine too long into too many doors. Modern ones don't need to be pushed. They open and shut automatically."

"Sorry, but I don't get it."

"Well, I'll give you a hint. Mix Dancer is planning to make San Francisco a branch office. The big stuff will be back in New York."

"Branch or main, what difference does it make? Aren't you still president with a capital 'P'?"

"Wrong size, lower case. Dancer wanted a San Francisco office. I had the contacts; he got the contracts. I've done my job as an opener. So what am I left with? A title, a desk, and a lot of papers to shuffle through."

For a moment I wondered if I'd been to blame, urging him on. But, as if Charlie had read my doubts, he added, "I've been lucky. I've worked during the good years. I've had my turn at bat. Now, I'm quitting before they call me out."

So, almost with a snap of the fingers Charlie said good-bye to the ad game. Perhaps, as he insisted, he had no regrets, but once more I chose to do the interpreting. Wouldn't he be lost, aimlessly walking down Montgomery Street in the mornings, spending his afternoons at the Bohemian Club, and waiting for the summer interval of the Grove encampment? It was then that I suggested we move to Sonoma. The change, I argued, would be good for him.

But was it I, or Charlie, who had sought this Walden Pond refuge in the Valley of the Moon?

XXII

LONG MAY THEY WAVE

WITHIN WEEKS we sold our home in San Francisco and found a modern ranch house in the Valley of the Moon, with what Charlie called modern inconveniences—a disposal that got jammed immediately, sliding glass windows so clear that Charlie almost crashed through a panel, and doors with hidden springs that we had to bang against and grope to find the openings.

The ranch house was off the main highway between the towns of Sonoma and Glen Ellen. A dirt road bordered with young fruit trees led to the entrance. There was an uncultivated terrace at the rear with one oak tree, a view of rolling hills, and stillness broken now and again by the moo of cows at three in the morning. Who could ask for anything more?

"Perfect," I kept repeating to Charlie. "A chance to commune with nature."

He smiled agreement and went off to commune with the members of the country club, while I was left to commune with Beulah, a two-hundred-pound woman I'd hired to help put our possessions into nooks and crannies where they didn't fit. Avidly I studied *House Beautiful* and *Sunset* magazines, sure that with a little remodeling our home would be as country charming as the glowing photographs promised. By the end of the week I was tired of the companionship of the butcher, the baker, and Beulah. And though I wouldn't admit it, I was tired of no other company than Charlie's.

I'd about had it on the day I came in the doorway juggling a sack of groceries to the tune of the noonday siren. Immediately I noticed the round table in the dining area set for three. My best dishes were on display and a bouquet of lilacs appeared to be growing right out of the crystal centerpiece.

"Who," I asked Beulah, my voice lilting in anticipation, "is coming for dinner?"

"Lunch," Beulah corrected, taking the groceries from me.

"Well, for lunch. Who's coming?"

"I am. Mr. McDougall invited me." And with a careless shrug that said "another little pound won't do me any harm," she beamed toward the kitchen. I followed her glance to see Charlie recessed behind the cupboards and the electric stove lit up like a pinball machine. He was deep into one of his original concoctions. My only clues were an opened sardine tin, a pot foaming at the mouth with noodles, and tomato paste bleeding on the counter. I don't recall the results. What I can't forget is that I spent most of the meal running between the kitchen and the dining room waiting on my husband and Beulah. I wasn't going to let him get away with it. No sooner had Beulah departed with a gracious "Deeelicious" than I attacked. "How could you?"

His smile was at its irritating best. "What could I do? Beulah said my cooking smelled so good."

By the end of the following week my social life began to improve. We were invited to an afternoon welcome party by one of our neighbors. Suddenly the hostess, a charming do-gooder, turned to the guests and asked, "How would you like to buy an American flag? Only $3.55. The money goes to 'Save the Road Runners.' "

I looked at Charlie who never minded spending a few cents here and more dollars there. I'd heard about the time when Batten's treasurer called him on the carpet to tell him he was responsible for half that month's expense account. In response, Charlie exploded, "Who in the hell had the guts to turn in the other half?" So what difference did $3.55 make?

"I would," I volunteered, and let Charlie fish the money out of his pocket.

Our hostess handed me a long carton and added, "There's a staff in there, too."

Back home, Charlie undid the carton, unfurled the flag, and fondled the red, white, and blue. "You know, this gives me an idea. Why not buy the California Bear flag, too, and fly them together?"

Yes, I agreed, that would be picturesque and make our home easy for visitors to find.

Well, the California flag with its special insignia cost $13.40. When I brought Charlie the staff on which to hoist the flags, he shook his head. The pole was not imposing enough for two flags. He consulted our contractor. What we needed, it seemed, was a twenty-foot pole made of Douglas fir, a type of wood that could give with the wind. The base should be of redwood, resistant to the elements. And, of course, we had to have a nylon cord and a gold-ball top piece. "Sure, sure," Charlie nodded, omitting to ask the cost.

Since this was Charlie's project, he chose the spot for Old Glory and the Bear—at the edge of our driveway within easy view of Highway 101. Once having indicated the location to the laborer who came early in the morning to dig, Charlie departed. The laborer dug four hours straight, then he knocked on the door. I opened it to see him dripping sweat from brow and chin. "All clay, lady," he said. "Maybe this will take another day."

By the time he'd finished, we had a hole five feet deep and five feet square practically at our front doorstep. Charlie assured me the hole could be easily filled. He neglected to mention the three hundred pounds of concrete the laborer said it would take to fill the hole.

On an afternoon late in November, Charlie hoisted our flags, with a hasty flip tied the cords to the hook at the base, and stepped back. "They look great. Make a fine landmark."

"A permanent one," I said, staring at the fresh cement. "You'll have to take the flags down each evening," I added, punishing him for the cost.

"I don't think so. Seems to me there's a new regulation for civilians."

I rushed for the almanac. "Says right here: 'It is the universal custom to display the flag only from sunrise to sunset.' "

"So what? This is *my* house, *my* property, and *my* flags. I'll make *my* own rules." With a final glance of admiration at the flying colors, he went into the house.

"You're as set as that concrete!" I shouted after him. He didn't turn his head. What was the use? Would I never learn? Might as well forget the whole thing. And I did, until the next morning when I wakened to the persistent ring of our doorbell. The spinster, who lived on the hill back of our house, stood with her beagle in our doorway. Both were panting. "Oh, dear," she said, "which one of our national leaders has passed on?" The hound and she turned mournful gazes toward our flags. They had slipped in the night to half staff. Already our telephone was ringing. I let it ring and ran for Charlie. In his anxiety to adjust the knot, he used his pocket knife and cut the nylon cord. Charlie had reversed the rule.

The flags had come down at sunrise instead of sunset. A new cord had to be purchased.

By now we had spent exactly $114.12 on our flags. Not such a great sum, Charlie reminded me, considering all the extra cupboards I wanted installed, to say nothing about landscaping.

Landscaping! I'd almost forgotten that our gardener was arriving at noon today from San Francisco to go over the plans drawn by the local nursery. She arrived on the dot, a precise little woman with British accent. First she inspected the terrain at the rear of the house. Carefully she measured the ground while consulting the blueprint in her hand. "This will make a lovely garden," she said. "Your oak tree is in good condition and the landscaping is in keeping with the Sonoma countryside." Next she turned her attention to the young fruit trees bordering the driveway in front. Once more she nodded her approval. "The trees are healthy and well planted. I have only one suggestion to make."

"What?" Charlie asked.

"In summer," she said, "you'll find it quite hot. By your parking space you should plant a row of shade trees."

"Excellent idea," Charlie agreed.

"Of course," said our gardener in clipped accent, "you won't object to moving your flagpole six feet to the right."

It couldn't have been more than two weeks after I'd had my fill of flags up to the sky and down again when Charlie opened the ranch house door and whistled. I came toward him to recognize the beam of a creative morning in his eyes. Under his arm he held a canvas.

"Let me see." I reached for the canvas.

With a teasing gesture he withheld it from view, then turned it toward me.

I expected to see the outline of an oak or perhaps a curve

of seascape. I certainly wasn't prepared for this: a colored poster illustration of a citrus moon dangling in a purple sky.

"What do you think?"

"Colors are good. Only I'm puzzled. Not representational, not pop art and not your usual style."

"It's a design for a flag—a flag for the Valley of the Moon. "Do you realize," he said, rushing from visualization to realization, "there are flags for every country, but there's never been one for Jack London's Valley of the Moon?"

I didn't want to dampen his enthusiasm by mentioning the Valley of the Moon was not a country, or even a state, so I studied the painting while he went on. "I know a flag company in San Francisco. I'll send them the design. They can make it up and we can have a ceremony with the lady mayor, our neighbors, and the residents of Sonoma to celebrate. I'll make shish kebab. You can make Caesar salad and Denny's Club can serve the beer."

I held the fort against him for a while. Nor did it do my cause any good to hum "Oh say can you see." There was no escaping the celebration. The Valley of the Moon flag was hoisted up our pole by the lady mayor, not at sunrise or at sunset, but to the blast of the noon siren. The local photographers and press were there. So were the freeloaders. All stood at attention while the band, drowned out by the siren, played "Sonoma Moon." No sooner had the flag reached its pinnacle next to the Stars and Stripes and the California Bear than there was a unanimous dash for refreshments. Charlie donned his chef's cap and barbecued pounds of shish kebab, while the bartender from Denny's turned on the spigots and let flow the beer from their kegs. I ran back and forth between the guests with wooden bowls filled with salads and with baskets loaded with garlic-scented French bread.

Once the last guest had departed, Charlie settled himself into a beach chair, a beer can in hand, while I picked up pieces of broken glass and gathered leftover paper plates.

"What can I do to help?" he asked.

"Help?" I yelled back, slamming down the lid on the overflowing garbage can. "Go find yourself a flag psychiatrist."

XXIII

END OF
A PASTORAL "IDLE"

I T WAS fall again. The leaves on the trees had turned to burnt orange. Inside the ranch house I shivered a little with the first chill in the air. I was not, I decided, a woman for all seasons. At least not in the Valley of the Moon.

While I waited for Charlie, who'd been gone nearly all afternoon working on a painting of an old stone winery, I lit the fire. When Charlie walked in, he did not have a canvas in his hand.

"What happened to your painting?" I asked.

"I wasn't satisfied." He came over and plumped down on the sofa next to me. "Couldn't get the darn thing into perspective."

Perspective? Who, I wondered, ever gets a true perspective? For a while we watched the flames, then without willing it I blurted, "Charlie, I want to go back to San Francisco. I want to die there."

"Die? You mean we want to *live* there."

"You too? And I thought—"

195

Charlie smiled. "One hand washes the other."

Within weeks we moved to a compact apartment atop Telegraph Hill to *live*, as Charlie said, in San Francisco.

But who calls the shots? Now Charlie, too, is gone. Not in the words "Until death do you part," because death does not part, not if you are left with all those sad funny things you shared.

As I stand today at the living-room windows, I hear the wail of the foghorns. Their familiar moan brings back the past, when in Mannie's day there were no bridges spanning the bay, no jet-propelled ferryboats churning angry plumes of spray, only the slow-moving ferries whose brass arms pumped up and down in leisurely progress to the weather-beaten, creosote-smelling piers of Oakland Mole. I feel myself back again in the city I'd known from childhood, hardly aware of the changes that have taken place during the years: the bay whose outlines have been pushed back by fill, the Barbary Coast replaced by nudie and encounter parlors, the rising skyline of a little New York with a pyramid towering over the financial district. But beneath the high rises, the plump Victorian houses still remain in smug historic permanence, and beneath all the surface changes, the heart of the city is still vital and buoyant. San Francisco has survived the bumps and grinds of change as it did the earth-shaking ones of the 1906 disaster.

Time doesn't march on or roll on; it skids by. One by one all the Brandenstein (Bransten) brothers have gone, like so many little Indians on a fence. Mannie was one of the first, and Eddie the last—maybe because he wanted to see his baby, rice, grow up healthy, which it has right here in the United States.

Now, fifty years later, Mannie's ship of business rides high on the waves once more. My brother Joe is retired hon-

orary chairman of the board of MJB, and retired or not, he
is as active as ever and keeps an eye on the hotel-restaurant
division. With pride he says, "We are the last, large, family-
owned coffee concern in the country." There is a silent
efficiency about the new company, no longer a partnership,
but a corporation run with less excitement. The air is divested
of its fragrant coffee aroma by antipollution laws. No longer
do men like Sandy and Altman run the sales force. No longer
does Mr. Hartwick drive furiously to cope with the brothers'
conflicting errands. A former bank guard drives the company
car as if conveying sacks of gold. Miss Alanson, plump
Sweetie-Pie, has long since bowed out to a faceless computer.
The rarefied atmosphere reminds me of when, as a child, I
asked Dad to "change tunes."

Yes, the tune has changed, but the "Brand" plays on.
And as time passes, Mannie is remembered. Not at the end,
when he was frail, but all through the early years, the man in
his strength and wisdom. Little inconsequential things—the
scent of cigarettes, eucalyptus oil, the parting of a theater
curtain, the sight of a tilted derby—are touchstones of yesterday's laughter. And when you drive down the steep Clay
Street grade that passes between old Chinatown and the new,
you see high on a cracked brick wall, faded but still legible,
the legend: MJB WHY?

And what about Charlie? Hadn't he, like Mannie, who
wore all the hats, lived in a time when he was free to splash
the canvas with bold strokes? Had he kept at it, hanging on,
wouldn't he, like a bonsai, have been dwarfed and reshaped
to fit today's ad pattern with departmentalization, subliminal
approach, status pull, and all the rest?

I glance from the window to Charlie's desk where the
medal he received at the Batten anniversary party so many
years ago stands framed. A shaft of light breaks through the
mid-afternoon fog and catches the inscription: "Our Doubts
are Traitors. . . ."

Suddenly I recall once telling Charlie, "Don't take a drink till the sun goes over the yardarm." With a smile, he replied, "Don't say don't to me. Somewhere the sun is over the yardarm."

I walk over to the small bar in the corner of the room and mix myself a martini.

Ruth Bransten McDougall is a native San Franciscan, educated in local schools until her college days at Vassar (class of '24). She has lived in California ever since, raising a family and writing advertising copy, a newspaper column, and freelance articles for magazines such as *California Living* and *San Francisco Magazine*. She lives on Telegraph Hill, overlooking her favorite city, and is presently at work on her next book.